The Greatest Secret

God's Law of Attraction for Lasting
Happiness, Fulfillment,
Health, and Abundance in Life

RON MCINTOSH

WHITE STONE BOOKS

12 11 10 09 08   2 3 4 5 6 7 8 9 10

The Greatest Secret

God's Law of Attraction for Lasting Happiness, Fulfillment, Health, and Abundance in Life
ISBN 1-59379-119-4
Copyright © 2007 by Ron McIntosh

Published by White Stone Books
P.O. Box 2835
Lakeland, Florida 33806

DEDICATION

I want to take a moment to thank some people who helped make this book a reality. Writing is hard work, and it is a collaborative effort.

I first want to thank Sue Scoggin for her tireless effort to press through to finish this manuscript. Your extra effort—to do it and then to do it over again—is one of the reasons this book is in print.

I also want to thank Susi Taylor whose constant encouragement caused me to press through when I thought maybe the price wasn't worth it. Friends are so important.

Most of all, I dedicate this work to my wife and family. Without their encouragement and support, I could never have taken the long hours, often away from them, to accomplish this task. Judy's love is the greatest cornerstone in my life this side of heaven, and the very lives of my children David, and his new wife Shelly, Daniel, and Jonathan motivate me to love God more. Their devotion to Christ inspires me.

TABLE OF CONTENTS

FOREWORD

I have written on many subjects involving the power, role, and impact of the mind on the quality of life for mankind on planet earth. Throughout history many scholars, sages, philosophers, and gurus have explored the complex nature of the mind of man and its integration in the human equation of body, soul, and spirit.

King Solomon three thousand years ago summarized his conclusion on the matter in his well-quoted statement: "As a man thinks in his heart (mind) so is he." This simple statement is pregnant with profound truth and addresses the heart and essence of mankind's sojourn on earth. It has been long believed that the mind plays a pivotal role in the experience of life, and in every generation the subject is reintroduced with fresh perspectives.

This exceptional work by Ron McIntosh is one of the most profound, practical, principle-centered approaches to this subject I have read in a long time. The author's approach to this subject brings a fresh breath of air that captivates the heart and engages the mind of the reader. His ability to leap over complicated theological and metaphysical jargon and reduce complex theories to simple practical principles that the least among us could understand is amazing. This work will challenge the intellectual while embracing the laymen as it dismantles the mysteries of the soul of man and delivers the profound in simplicity.

Ron's engaging approach to the impact of your personal belief system, self-concept, and environment on your life and future awakens in the reader the untapped inhibiters that retard our personal development, and his antidotes empower us to rise above these self-limiting factors to a life of exploits in spiritual and mental advancement. The author also integrates into each chapter the time-tested precepts of biblical script, giving each principle a practical application to life, making the entire process people-friendly. At the end of each chapter, he provides personal exercises that allow us to immediately apply the principles to our lives, taking us beyond theory to practice.

This work is destined to become a classic and should be read by all who desire to break free from the restrictions of their past, embrace the lessons of the present, and pursue the opportunities and possibilities of the future. Every sentence of this book is pregnant with wisdom, and I enjoyed the mind-expanding experience of this exciting book. I admonish you to plunge into this ocean of the following pages and watch your life change for the better.

Dr. Myles E. Munroe
Nassau, Bahamas
2007

INTRODUCTION

The idea for this writing was initiated by a pastor friend in the Grand Rapids, Michigan area. Paul called me and asked, "Have you heard about the book and DVD called *The Secret?*"

I responded, "I haven't heard of it."

Paul added, "The reason I read it, is because it teaches something you introduced in our church several years ago, the 'Law of Attraction.' Read the book and tell me what you think."

Because of who I am (a Bible School Director) and because of what I do (travel and speak), there's always someone who is asking about the latest trend, philosophy or theology. It is no less so with the latest phenomena, *The Secret. The Secret* is the best-selling combo of the book and DVD. Millions of copies have been sold of the works espousing the "Law of Attraction."

The Law of Attraction, says, "like attracts like." If you see it in your mind, you're going to hold it in your hand. Everything coming to your life, you are attracting to your life, by your dominant thoughts.

This book is about the "secret" to "the secret." It is about the "greatest secret." *The Secret* draws or attracts from an impersonal universe. The "greatest secret" draws from a personal God. The "greatest secret" is knowing Jesus Christ as Lord and Savior. A relationship with a personal God puts you in touch with Kingdom laws that attract the manifestations of the Kingdom of Heaven. The law in which all laws culminate is the Law of Attraction. You attract to yourself people, ideas and resources according to your most dominant thoughts.

The "greatest secret" however, is a "secret" because it has been masked in mediocrity. A mediocre Christian is like false advertising. We come and say to people, "Jesus offers you abundant life," but our lifestyle belies our statement.

The term *abundant* means superabundant in quantity, superior in quality. We are to be a people who have superabundant love, joy, peace, faith, self-control, stability, prosperity (Proverbs 8:21), health, exciting relationships at every level and successful life. The greatest secret is that we, as believers, are to be productive at every level of life.

This is God's will (John 10:10, Ephesians 3:20, Joshua 1:8, Psalm 1:2, 3) yet, it is obvious that there is a gap between what we say we believe, and what we actually experience. It is a secret that is hidden because we often mirror other people's reflections, rather than God's system. Look at these statistics from the Barna Research Center:[1]

BEHAVIOR	BORN AGAIN CHRISTIANS	NON-CHRISTIANS
Watched MTV or a music channel last week	19%	24%
Donated money to non-profit organization last month	27%	23%
Volunteered time to help non-profit organization in the past week	29%	27%

Intentionally encouraged or complimented someone in the past week	86%	77%
Had a session with a professional counselor in the last year	70%	73%
Took drugs or medication prescribed for depression in the past year	7%	8%
Tried to influence someone's opinion on an issue in the past year	47%	49%
Watched "R" rated movie in the past 3 months	76%	87%
Watched "X" or "NC17" rated movie in the past 3 months	9%	16%
Participated in a chat room on the internet in the past year	8%	11%

If we are a part of the most powerful entity on the planet, why is there so little distinctiveness about who we are? Is success elusive, or is there something we don't know? Is there a secret that unlocks the door to productivity and the fulfillment (abundance) we so earnestly desire?

The greatest secret is the revelation of "keys" (laws) in God's Word to attract to yourself the blessing, which God so earnestly desires to imbue in your life. This is a secret because there is a gap represented by mediocrity and frustration, the gap between what you say you believe and what you experience. This is a secret to take you from where you are, to where you want to be.

It is only a secret because we have unwittingly overlooked it. As we reexamine the truth of scripture, prepare to experience abundance, real abundance—real abundance of feeling loved and fulfilled—abundance with real prosperity (giving and receiving in order to be a blessing to others), not just materialism. Real abundance is joy. Joy is not just an emotion guided by your circumstances. It is not just "joy because," but "joy regardless." Real abundance brings peace, and not just peace because of the lack of storms, but peace *in* the storms as well.

The greatest secret is about facing your present limitation and breaking every barrier. The greatest secret is about the effortless way to make your God-given dreams come true. It is time to experience abundant life. It may look a little different for every person, but love, joy, peace, and blessing are your "lot in life." Prepare to discover the *"real secret."* Why is this important? Philemon 6 says it this way: "That the communication (release or transfer-Greek)[2] of [your] faith may become effectual (productive; working or producing the desired effect)[3] by the acknowledging of every good thing [that] is in you in Christ Jesus."

In other words, the author is saying, there is a transfer of faith into our lives at salvation. The essence of faith is taking things desired to things possessed. It is a productive force that produces a desired effect. It comes as a result of recognizing the finished work of God in you at salvation (2 Corinthians 5:12, Hebrews 12:23, Colossians 2:9). The point is that the effectiveness of communicating our faith is most contingent on our ability to recognize who we are in Christ and to experience the benefits. People don't effectively communicate what they don't experience or are not productive in. It is essential to be productive in Kingdom laws and experience the blessing of the Kingdom of Heaven to effectively communicate the essence of the Gospel. It is time to experience God's blessing and abundance. Prepare to live a *life without limits!*

Chapter 1

THE REAL SECRET

AS I WALKED INTO AN interview, the host looked at me and said, "What is the greatest secret?"

Without hesitation I responded, the greatest secret is finding a real relationship with the God of the universe, through His Son. The reason it's a secret is it has been lost in the guise of religion. It has been lost in co-dependent people living vicariously through Christian celebrities, while hoping some magical secret will fall out of the sky and make all their dreams come true. The greatest secret was ignited in my life when I realized my salvation allowed me to "see" what the kingdom of God had for me (John 3:3). It was a Kingdom that took me beyond mere importance to real significance. Importance may bring recognition, but significance brings the true meaning to life.

I'm talking about significance in relationships, not simply connecting with another person, but relationships that have real meaning and inspire you to be your very best. We're talking about significance in your finances. You were blessed to be a blessing. It is difficult however, to help someone else if you are barely surviving yourself. Significance about how you feel about yourself. You can't truly love someone else, if you don't feel loved. Significance is important also in the realm of peace…it's not just peace when things go well, but *until* things go well. This significance isn't for temporal things alone, but it is a significance for eternity. People are not only looking for breakthroughs, but breakthroughs that have meaning to them. God grants prosperity, but adds no sorrow to it (Proverbs 10:22). People not only want success, but "good success" (Joshua 1: 8). It is success that brings increase, but not divorce, disharmony, broken hearts or empty lives with it. The greatest secret is the discovery that a relationship with God opens our eyes to see kingdom laws of love and provision beyond our wildest imaginations.

Rhonda Byrne in her runaway best seller *The Secret* begins by saying in essence "What if I told you there is a secret that has helped 1 percent of the population earn 96 percent of the world's wealth?"[1]

This is a secret that I actually learned about five years ago. However, I didn't learn to apply it consistently until about three months ago, or about the time I started writing this book. Since that time I've been watching my destiny unfold and my dreams come true in a remarkable way. It's a secret that once you submit to it, it will catapult you to the highest levels of success, fulfillment, and personal satisfaction that you would never have believed possible.

It is a secret called the **Law of Attraction.**

Recently, a quiet phenomenon has surrounded a DVD and book called *The Secret,* which expounds on the Law of Attraction. At this writing, millions of DVDs and books have been sold around the world. People are entrenched in a quest for productivity, meaning, and success in their lives.

I also had a strong desire to see the spiritual status quo and stagnation broken off of people's lives. I knew God's will was abundance, so I began a personal quest to help people find their greatest productivity and fulfillment.

MY QUEST

About five years ago I began asking some difficult questions about the productivity of believers and God's church. I asked myself, "If the Body of Christ is the most powerful entity on the planet, then why aren't we more distinguished from the world than we are? If Jesus promised abundance, why aren't more of His people experiencing it? If God's message is one of redemption and healing (See Isaiah 53:4, 5; Matthew 8:17; Luke 4:18, 19; 1 Peter 2:24), then why are so many Christians sick? If it is God's will to set people free, why are so many believers hopelessly bound by fears, insecurities, and addictions of every kind?" God wants us to experience harmonious and productive relationships, but the modern world we live in is full of divisions and strife (even in the church). God's will is for us to be successful in every area of our lives, but so many believers are mired in stagnation and defeat. Has success become elusive and complicated, or have we just missed something? Are we reaching our desires or getting what we don't want?

I began poring over Scripture for hours at a time, searching for an answer. As I examined verse after verse, I began to discover certain keys or kingdom laws to attract the kingdom of heaven to ourselves.

During this time I had lunch with a highly recognized Christian leader from Tulsa. In between bites of fried rice as we talked about the world and the church, he paused and looked across the table and said to me, "What do you think God is doing right now?"

After I had some brief interaction about what I was learning, I responded, "I believe God is showing us keys to unlock the kingdom of heaven in greater ways than we've ever known before." I left that meeting knowing that God was showing me the keys to help people walk out of lives mired in mediocrity and step into new levels of abundance. I was deeply committed to communicating these truths with others.

When I walked into my staff meeting the next day, God gave me an illustration to communicate this truth. I looked across the room at one of my key staff members and said, "Liz, I want you to go outside the door to this room. I'm going to lock the door behind you. Here's the key to the room. I want you to unlock the door and come back in." After some whimsical banter and stares from some of the other staff members, she agreed to humor me and left the room.

I locked the door behind her and said loud enough for her to hear me, "Liz, use the key to unlock the door and come back in."

After several moments of trying, she said, "I can't get the door to open."

"Try harder," I replied.

She tried to get the key to turn in the lock for a while longer, but the key wouldn't work. So I encouraged her not to give up but keep trying. She plodded away for a few more moments, but the key still wouldn't work. By that time, I could tell my staff was beginning to wonder what was going on. Liz made several more attempts and finally declared in frustration, "No matter how hard I try, I can't get the door to open. I think you gave me the wrong key."

"You're absolutely right," I told her. "I gave you the wrong key."

When I opened the door and the meeting resumed, I had everyone's attention. It was the perfect opportunity for me to train my staff on what God had been teaching me concerning the keys to unlock heaven's provision for our lives.

This little demonstration is a picture of what the church is experiencing today. Many believers are on the other side of the locked door. They believe God should bless them because they are sincere and are trying hard. They tell themselves, "After all, I go to church twice a week, I read my Bible on occasion, and I'm making an effort."

Here is the important fact I don't want you to miss. It doesn't matter how hard you try or how sincere you are, you can't open the door unless you have the right key.

In this hour in which we are living, God is supernaturally revealing His keys to bring about productivity in people's lives. People are tired of a Gospel, no matter how true it is, that they can't get to work. Matthew 16:19 says it this way: "I will give you the keys of the kingdom of heaven; whatever you bind on earth will be ("must already be," Amplified version) bound in heaven, and whatever you loose on earth, will be loosed ("must be already loosed," Amplified version) in heaven." Somehow, the church has managed to reduce the magnitude of this verse to semantics in prayer like "I bind the devil," etc. While there is some truth to this thought process, this passage is more about "keys" or laws that govern access or *attract* the manifestation of the kingdom of heaven. The kingdom of heaven (or the kingdom of God) is God's rule. It is also the combination of the location and resources of God and the system by which you access them in your life. Accessing kingdom resources allows believers to dominate their environment (Genesis 1:26) and establish God's rule and reign on earth.[2]

Biblical language expert, Dr. William McDonald, suggests that the concept of the kingdom of heaven equates to the supernatural element of God.[3] God's rule (kingdom) occurs primarily when a person's heart is under the influence of the grace from kingdom laws (principles). The supernatural rule of the kingdom on earth is activating God's supernatural provision by yielding to it in our hearts. Thus, the essence of the kingdom is the unseen, coming to the seen, so He (God) can be on the scene.

Jesus is saying that His kingdom is one of order and operates by divinely appointed laws (keys). Once you understand these laws and operate in them, you will attract the kingdom's provision for your life. Once the kingdom of heaven is released (loosed) in a person's life, it will in turn stop (bind) the kingdom of darkness (or the devil's work). However, it doesn't do any good to give keys to someone if they don't know how to use them. I can have a ring full of keys (principles or laws), but if I don't know what doors they fit, they are useless.

As I look around, there are people of all kinds who are feeling a sense of lack in their lives. People are hungry for a truth to unlock the doors to productivity and fulfillment. People are looking for a secret key, which has been hidden, that will open the door to living a life without limits.

It is the spiritual vacuum that has caused countless millions to delve into *The Secret* for an answer.

THE LAW OF ATTRACTION

The main thrust of the Law of Attraction as found in *The Secret* is that "like attracts like." Everything coming to your life you are attracting into your life. It is attracted to you by the images you are holding in your mind.[4] *The Secret* proposes that if we obey certain laws in the universe, those laws will yield the opulence of the universe. According to this work, it is not a complicated process. Once you've learned "the secret," then a whole new realm of possibility opens to you.

The dominant law is the Law of Attraction. Whether it is positive or negative, everything you are experiencing in your life you have attracted to yourself. And the way you attract it to yourself is through your pattern of thinking. Whatever your dominant thoughts are, that is what you will attract to your life.[5]

The question is, "Is this New Age 'mumbo jumbo,' or the truth so many people are looking for to bring productivity to their lives?" Reaction to this book ranges from "poppycock," to "it's heresy," to "I love the principle and Oprah" (as seen on her TV show). The Law of Attraction in *The Secret* is based on a certain philosophical premise from quantum physics. However, you don't have to be a quantum physicist to understand what they are saying. The idea is that everything in the universe—from the vast galaxies to the atoms that make up the most infinitesimal molecule—is simply energy vibrating in harmony. The conclusion is that nothing is solid. It is only energy vibrating at a certain level. It feels solid because its molecules are vibrating.[6]

What we see in the physical sense is vibrational interpretation. What you see, you see because your eyes translate vibration. All five senses, then, are activated by vibration. The ultimate premise of this philosophy is that the most potent form of energy is thought.[7] You can harness all other forms of energy through thought. Thus, you can attract to yourself health, wealth, and all forms of abundance from the universe simply by transforming your thoughts to agree with this Law of Attraction.

So, is *The Secret's* Law of Attraction New Age "mumbo jumbo"? Yes! (And, no.) It is New Age, or what many call today "New Thought." It is also reflective of God's laws that He has sovereignly placed in the universe. It is primarily an imitation of God's truth. The Law of Attraction is not simply some visualization of fantasy, then sprinkling of some pixie dust, and magically your wildest imaginations appear. God's Law of Attraction is about renewing your mind, establishing your heart, and transforming your personal belief system in such a way that you attract His kingdom to yourself through faith in Him.

So that there's no lack of understanding, let's separate fact from fiction.

❦

There are kingdom laws that will attract God's provision.

The fact is, *The Secret's Law of Attraction* is closer to "The Force" of Star Wars than to the truth of scripture, but there is truth to the Law of Attraction. We are not attracting energy from our impersonal universe, but provision willingly given by a Father in heaven who lives to give good gifts to His children (Luke 11:13). It is not the universe that provides us with abundance, but God Himself, governed by His immutable principles that He has set in place. It certainly takes less faith to believe in a personal God longing to have a relationship with His creation than to somehow believe that a non-personal universe is somehow providing all that we need.

God's Law of Attraction is not some humanistic endeavor (though there are universal laws). It is teaching people how to renew their minds, establish their hearts, and transform their personal belief system to align themselves to God's truths and manifest His provision for mankind.

This is not Metaphysics (after or beyond physics, which may include mind over matter), but learning to apply the keys to the kingdom. God's Law of Attraction is not some New Age mantra to twist the arm of the universe to give up its abundance, but the law of a loving God to bless you beyond comprehension.

The Holy Spirit is attracting to you people, ideas (revelations), and resources according to your transformed belief system (Romans 12:2). Religion rejects it. New Age "science" perverts it. Humanists attempt to demythologize it. God's laws (7,700 of them) seek to destroy the boundaries (the limitations) of your life. This book is not simply about discovering what is wrong, but about helping people understand God's keys to bring productivity and blessing into their lives.

The Secret's Law of Attraction says, "Like attracts like." A more accurate definition would look more like this: "You attract to yourself people, ideas, and resources according to your most dominant thoughts."[8] From a practical standpoint, what you focus on, give your attention to, or renew your mind to, you attract to yourself (you're likely to create as reality). What you focus on the longest becomes the strongest! It is what John Maxwell, an expert on motivational leadership, calls the Law of Magnetism (you are a human magnet). The fact is, once your mind is renewed, your heart is established, and your life is congruent with kingdom principles, you will attract the kingdom of heaven unto yourself.

This is not a book on newtonian physics, quantum physics, or metaphysical philosophy. It is about transforming your thinking to kingdom laws, so that you can attract the kingdom by faith. There will always be claims that this kind of thought is selfish. Somehow it is more "noble" to be poor or unproductive. The fact is the Law of Attraction is not selfish in its essence. The effect of success or prosperity is simply a reflection of the attitude of one's heart.

It is much like the movie *Hollow Man.* In this movie, Kevin Bacon plays Sebastian Caine, a brilliant scientist who has developed a serum that can make you completely invisible. Sebastian decides to inject himself with the serum. Once he becomes invisible he does some detestable selfish acts. It is important to note, however, that it wasn't the invisibility that caused the selfish acts. The invisibility simply revealed what was already in his heart.

Similarly, the attitude of our hearts determines how blessing affects us. We can attract either positives or negatives to our lives. Proverbs 23:7 grants great insight on life, conduct, and even what we think about: "For as he (a man) thinks in his heart, so is he…." (NKJV). We must not only guard our hearts (Proverbs 4:23) to experience God's blessing, but we must change our way of thinking. It is more important to guard our hearts than to block it from blessings. When God called Abraham to begin a relationship with Him, He had to change Abraham's view of himself. He said: "I will make you into a great nation and I will bless you; I will make your name great and you will be a blessing" (Genesis 12:2). Think about it. Abraham was standing out looking up at the dark sky, staring at the millions of stars that sparkled in the heavens, and then in the stillness of the night, the God of all creation said, "'Look up at the heavens and count the stars—if indeed you can count them.'" Then He said to him, "'So shall your offspring be'" (Genesis 15:5). What do you think was going through Abraham's mind? You can be sure it jolted his thinking to a whole new level of who this marvelous God was. He is the same God who wants to do more than we can ever imagine if we'll only change our thinking and learn His keys (Ephesians 3:20). Then God said to him, "…and all peoples on earth will be blessed through you" (Genesis 12:3). He was blessed to be a blessing. The whole attitude of a renewed mind is abundance *and* generosity. It is productivity to receive from God and to give to others.

I want to show you the "effortless" way that will bring what Jesus calls abundance into your life. The Law of Attraction is not about Tinkerbell and pixie dust, or that visualization magically turns your innermost desires into reality. It is about learning to transform your thinking into "faith," which will attract God's greatest blessing. Like most imitations of truth by New Age or other sects, *The Secret's* definition of the Law of Attraction is simply a distortion of the biblical truth. It is important, however, not to throw the baby out with the bath water, but to isolate and implement the part that is truth in such a way as to maximize the blessing God intends for us.

The Greatest Secret is about God's "extreme makeover." It is a radical transformation that supernaturally comes from the inside out. Once you conform your thinking to kingdom laws, every aspect of your life will change. The main reason Jesus came to earth was to seek and save that which is lost. He also came to make earth like heaven. That is why He taught us to pray, "Your kingdom come, your will be done on earth as it is in heaven" (Matthew 6:10). Notice it is God's intent to bring heaven to earth, but it is not automatic. There are thinking patterns that have to change, laws that have to be learned and operated in. That's why He gave His disciples (you and me) the keys to the kingdom (Matthew 16:19).

This is further reinforced in Psalm 115:16. "The highest heavens belong to the LORD, but the earth he has given to man." So when people say, "If God's in charge on earth, He's sure making a mess of things," the fact is, God is not in charge of earth. Man is in charge of the earth. And the way we get heaven to earth is by operating in the keys of the kingdom of heaven.

In Genesis 1:26, God sets forth this biblical precedent: "Then God said, 'Let us make man in our image, in our likeness, and let them rule…over all the earth.'" First God says, "Let us (the Godhead) make man in our image and likeness." The image of God is His nature, inborn character, innate disposition, inherent tendencies of a person, instincts or desires.[9] The term *likeness* means "function or characteristic action."[10]

God made man with His inherent tendencies and ability to function, take dominion, or dominate the earth (his environment). This passage reveals what I call the Four Laws of Genesis 1:26:

FOUR LAWS OF GENESIS 1:26

1. Legal authority to dominate and rule the earth was given to mankind (Psalm 115:16; Matthew 6:10).

2. God did not include Himself in the legal authority structure over earth.

3. Any influence or interference from the supernatural realm on earth is only legal through mankind. This means any supernatural forces, heavenly or demonic. Satan only has authority in the New Covenant where man relinquishes it.

4. God has made Himself subject to His own law and will not violate it.[11]

In other words, God made man to rule the visible world through the invisible realm by attracting God's kingdom to earth. The conclusion from these "keys" is that legal right and authorization for God to interfere in earth's affairs must be through a man.[12] When a man or woman operates in kingdom laws, he or she is authorizing or attracting the kingdom of God to manifest itself on the earth. This is why God says in Isaiah, "…concerning the work of my hands, command ye me…" (Isaiah 45:11, KJV). It's not that we are to order God around. After all, the Bible says He is our "shield and buckler" (Psalm 35:2), not our shield and butler. What He means is, concerning the things He has accomplished, command Him or authorize Him to manifest them.

It is interesting to note that the predominant title given to Jesus in the New Covenant is not Son of God (over forty references), but Son of Man (over ninety references). The reason for this is that God needed a man on the earth to use His keys to accomplish His will on earth. Jesus came to restore to mankind the authority and dominion that Adam gave to satan. By renewing our minds to kingdom laws, we create new dominant thoughts. These, in turn, transform our heart and our personal belief system (faith), which ultimately authorize the kingdom of heaven to manifest itself.

The Law of Attraction in God's kingdom attracts to itself, by the Holy Spirit, people, ideas (revelations), and resources of heaven according to our most dominant thoughts. The question is, how does it work? The "secret" to the secret is renewing our minds. Renewing our minds is God's "extreme makeover."

KEYS

The "secret" to a productive life is the Law of Attraction.

The Law of Attraction says, "Like attracts like." You attract to yourself people, ideas, and resources according to your most dominant thoughts.

According to Matthew 16:19, the "greatest secret" is that you attract the kingdom of heaven to yourself, according to your renewed thinking.

You don't attract the kingdom of heaven because you're trying hard, but because you use the keys (laws) of the kingdom of heaven.

The Secret's Law of Attraction differs from the kingdom's Law of Attraction. *The Secret* says that you attract what you need from the energy of an impersonal universe. The kingdom of heaven allows you to attract from all the provision God has already accomplished through Jesus.

Operating in kingdom laws allows you to take dominion and to dominate your environment with an authority backed by heaven.

Chapter 2

THE SECRET TO THE SECRET

God's Extreme Makeover

AT THE END of 2004, I read an article about the top television shows that year. Six out of the top ten rated shows were "reality" series shows. It is a genre that has literally captivated viewing audiences around the world. Shows like *Survivor, American Idol, The Apprentice, The Amazing Race,* and *Fear Factor* were among the most watched programming. None of these shows, however, was more dominant than *Extreme Makeover.* It's not more dominant because it was the highest rated TV show, but because there are so many derivations of this one single concept. There was *Extreme Makeover, Extreme Makeover Home Edition, Trading Spaces, The Swan,* and the list goes on and on. People are fixated on changing themselves.

One show in particular fascinated me, though I actually never saw a complete episode. It was called *The Swan.* The idea of this series was to select very homely women and give them a total makeover free of charge. The winner for each week would get to compete in a beauty pageant at the end of the year.

I was flipping through the stations one day, when a commercial for *The Swan* caught my attention. A panel of experts posted a most unflattering picture of a woman in shorts and a "crop" top to a board for observation. A host would ask, "What needs to be done for this woman?" Various experts took a black marker and began to circle areas of need. In this particular commercial, they circled her forehead, cheeks, chin, nose, and lips. As they moved to the body, they talked about certain augmentation and then liposuction…liposuction…liposuction.

Shortly after seeing this commercial, I read an article in *USA Today.* The article had a "before" picture and an "after" picture of women from *The Swan.* One woman had endured twenty-three separate surgeries and had been confined to a wheelchair for eight days. I was fascinated by what they were trying to accomplish. Later that season, I did catch the last fifteen minutes of the finale—the beauty pageant. As they were calling the women for their final interview question in true pageant format, they would post the "before" picture of each contestant. I must say the transformation was astonishing. In most cases, you couldn't tell if it was the same woman or not.

It was amazing to watch the extremes these women went to in order to find "transformation." They pursued an "outward" beauty that would make them feel better about themselves. I believe most of us need to learn to be happy with who we are and make the best of it we can. (I neither condemn nor endorse the process; it is a choice.) My point is simple. God's Extreme Makeover primarily comes from the inside out.

Your outside world does reflect your inward world. This is why two people can sit and listen to the same principles and one person is transformed and the other is not. Why is it that of all the people who go to seminars of any kind, less than 10 percent ever apply anything they hear? (This is even after they have spent big dollars for it.) You are where you are today because of the decisions you've made up to this point. Your outside life will directly correspond to your inward life. At this moment, you are manifesting in your life what you, truly believe on the inside.

Be honest with yourself and ask the hard questions. Are you satisfied with your life, your marriage, your family, your career? If life has thrown its share of disappointments your way, *it is not too late to change all of that.* God is ready and waiting with all of heaven's resources to help you. Now, renewing your mind, establishing your heart, and transforming your personal belief system is not the simple memorization of truth. It means transforming your total decision-making process. Once truth is solidified in your heart, it allows you the freedom to obey God's laws.

Secular writer Brian Tracy identified groupings of principles he calls laws. As I was thinking about what he wrote, I suddenly realized there were six biblical laws to success that make up the process of faith.

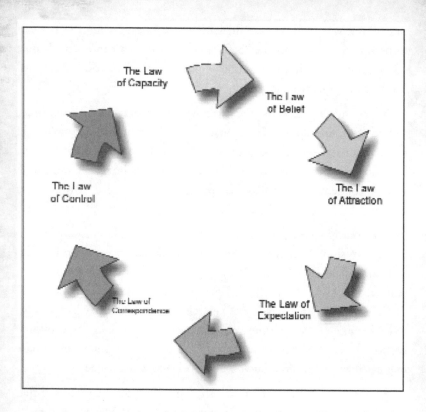

Here is what these laws look like:

The Law of Capacity: A person can only receive from God in direct correlation to his *capacity* to receive from God.

The Law of Control: People are positive in life to the extent they are in control of their lives.[1]

The Law of Belief: What you believe in your heart with confidence becomes your reality.[2] Everyone manifests what they believe. They either manifest abundance or scarcity.

The Law of Expectation: What you expect in your heart with conviction becomes self-fulfilling prophecy. Your steps are literally ordered by your expectations.[3]

The Law of Attraction: You attract unto yourself people, ideas, and resources according to your most dominant thoughts.[4] This is the process of manifestation in your life. This law causes things that are *potential* to become *actual.* All other laws gather at this law.

The Law of Correspondence: Your outside world corresponds directly to your inner world. In other words, what is without, is what is within.[5] All productive manifestation in your life is the result of your inner world, which is the result of a renewed mind, an established heart, and a transformed personal belief system.

❧

I have a brilliant friend from Huntsville, Alabama, by the name of Dr. Jim Richards. One day he was sharing with me how God's laws are reflected in natural laws. If you understand how natural laws work, you will understand how God's laws work. Romans 1:20 shows us this process: "For since the creation of the world, God's invisible qualities—his eternal power and Divine nature—have been clearly seen, being understood from what has been made…." In other words, nature's laws are simply a reflection of God's eternal laws. We can see this from certain laws of physics.

The Law of Entropy is a basic law that says things left unattended tend toward chaos. Isn't that true for most of our lives as well? We have serious issues we're trying to deal with, but we often hope they'll just go away if we ignore them long enough. The truth is that problems don't go away by ignoring them. In reality, they tend toward chaos. Yard work doesn't go away by ignoring it; the weeds only get worse. In the same way, your self-limiting beliefs don't simply disappear overnight by themselves. Once they are lodged in your subconscious mind, they work automatically to make those negative beliefs come to pass. Unfortunately, these thoughts often sabotage us and leave our lives in mediocrity or, worse, total chaos.

Another law is the *Law of Cause and Effect.* This law states that everything happens for a reason. Nature is neutral. It doesn't favor one person over another. Conversely, if anyone learns to operate in God's laws, they will work for them. So many people believe these laws only work for celebrities and the rich and famous, and not for common people. But that is not what God says. He is no respecter of persons. He honors faith wherever He finds it. In these days, He's raising up people who are revealing His secret: *you can be radically transformed by His laws and experience a new level of living.*

We can find another example in physics called the *Law of Hysteresis. Hysteresis* is the tendency of material to revert back to its original shape once the pressure changing it is removed. In psychology, it is called "setpoints," or self-limiting beliefs. When we hear a new truth, we change for a season. Then when the pressure of that word is removed, we revert back to our old lifestyles. God intends for you not only to be changed for a season, but to be transformed into new levels of achievement and productivity forever.

Another law, the *Law of Motion,* states that anything in motion stays in motion, unless acted upon by an opposite and equal force. If I were to roll a ball on a flat plain, it would roll forever, unless acted upon by a contrary force, such as gravity and friction. Similarly, in your life there are certain negative traits that are in motion and will continue to be, unless they are acted upon by an opposite force. Things you want changed don't just disappear. All change for good must be intentional. You must cooperate with the Holy Spirit with your will and target certain beliefs, identify them, disassociate yourself from them, and apply the antidote of new truths. As you apply new empowering beliefs, your life will jump to a new level. To move forward in kingdom growth, you must literally increase your capacity to receive from God. And that depends on the type of person you are.

Stephen Scott, in his profound book *Mentored by a Millionaire,* suggests there are four kinds of people in life:[6]

Drifters are basically people who go with the flow of life, allowing life to throw at them whatever it chooses. About 50 percent of people comprise this category.

Pursuers are basically people who pursue a dream until they meet an obstacle and then back off. About 25 percent of people make up this category.

Achievers are people who set lofty goals and achieve some of their dreams, but rarely achieve significant or extraordinary dreams. About 24.99 percent fall in this category.

Super-Achievers are those who have acquired their master strategies and skills to be successful in virtually every venue of their lives. They do the extraordinary. If your math is very good, that leaves about .01 percent.

Now, notice a few things. Jesus said, "I have come that you might have life and have it more abundantly."[7] He has come that you might have life and have it as a super-achiever. However, only about .01 percent are able to appropriate it. John 10:10 tells us that God desires a life of abundance for His children. In fact, the term *abundance* means "super-abundant in quantity, superior in quality, excess, surplus, excel, superfluous, or extreme."[8] God intends for us to tap into a life of productivity if we'll simply understand His laws of achievement.

Noted psychologist Martin Seligman wrote a book called *Learned Optimism*. In the book Seligman introduces the idea of "Learned Helplessness." The idea of "Learned Helplessness" is that you feel helpless to change your circumstances.[9] It is what Paul calls "strongholds" in 2 Corinthians 10:4. A stronghold is when you feel powerless to change something, though it is contrary to the will of God. It is when people hope something will change, but their past environments or experiences indicate the opposite. A false inner personal belief system will squash any sense that things will ever change, or that you can control your destiny.

THE SECRET REVEALED

If the Law of Attraction attracts people, ideas, and resources according to my most dominant thoughts, then how do I create new dominant thoughts that line up with God's kingdom provision? How do I create the intentional renewed thinking to attract the kingdom of heaven? How do I obtain a *new perspective* that will break the self-limiting beliefs that have held me back and launch me into living a life without limits?

The importance of perspective can be seen in a letter written by a young college student to her parents. You might want to read this as if it's your daughter writing to you.

Dear Mom and Dad:

I haven't made many friends, but I met a boy. He's not going to school and can't find a job, but he is doing better now that he has been released from prison. He didn't have a place to live, so he moved in with me. After all, we're going to need a home for the baby. Dad, you'll be glad to hear it's a boy. Turn the letter over for the P.S.

A gamut of raw emotions ran through these parents' minds. The mother began to sob, and the father just sat there in a daze, shaking his head. All their lives they had only wanted the best for their daughter. The father had worked hard so she could get a good education and learn a career. And now she had married a criminal and was pregnant. Everything had gone wrong. After a few moments, they turned the letter over and read the *P.S.*

> *P.S. None of this is true! But I did get a "C" in English and a "D" in Humanities and I need more money.*

Now that will change your perspective. Biblical laws are all about gaining a new quality and dimension in life. It is only when we make biblical truth and God's view of us our main focus that we will be able to change our perspective.

The Law of Attraction works from the dominant thoughts in your mind or heart. *The Secret* states, "If you see it in your mind, you'll hold it in your hand."[10] "Thoughts become things."[11] A predominant thought is like a magnet and attracts to its nature."[12] "The Law of Attraction is working whether you believe it or not."[13]

God's secret says that you attract the kingdom of heaven according to the dominant thoughts of your heart and mind. You are not attracting an impersonal force to give you what you need. You are entering into an amazing relationship with a God whose eternal truths and power can catapult you into a dimension of living that far exceeds anything you could ever imagine. So how do we create a dominant, renewed thought process that lines up with the abundant provision that God has available for us? Romans 12:2 NKJV, gives us the four key principles for provision by the renewing of our mind:

> *Do not be conformed to this world, but be transformed by the renewing of your mind, that you may prove what is the good, and acceptable and perfect will of God.*

PRINCIPLE # 1
"DO *NOT* BE CONFORMED"

The first principle is, do *not* be conformed to the world or to this world's system. Conformed is a fascinating word. It comes from two words: *con,* which means "with or together with"[14] and *form,* which means "shape, way or pattern of doing something."[15] *Conformed* in this verse means we do not want to be together with the way or pattern of doing something of the world or this world's system.

Why does the writer give such a stern warning? He knew that if you operate according to a particular system, all you can ever produce is what is natural to that system. In other words, you will attract whatever system you are part of. Paul wanted to show the limitation of the world's system and how to tap into God's kingdom.

The "world's system" is a thought process that is alienated from God's system of thought[16] or is a reflection of the age in which we're living.[17] Greek scholar Kenneth Wuest says the world's system is the thoughts, opinions, maxims, speculations, or people who operate outside of God's system. God has implanted many of His laws in the world. Thus, the world's system does have the ability to have productivity. It cannot, however, access the supernatural provision of God or find peace and fulfillment apart from circumstances going right. This is why there are people in the world's system who have success, but sometimes it is not what the Bible calls "good success." Good success is prosperity without sorrow (Proverbs 10:22). Good success has increase without family decimation, etc. Wittingly or unwittingly, we all are influenced in some measure by the thought processes reflective of this age in which we're living. (Obviously, there are multitudes of believers who are unwittingly in the world's system. This understanding of success is not simply about religion, but about learning to operate in the fullness of God's system.) Romans 6:16 indicates that the one I yield to is the one I obey. In other words, if I submit to the devil's system, I attract what that system offers. If I obey God, I attract what His kingdom offers.

Let me give you an example. If someone cuts me off on the street, and I react by anger or rage, I am attracting or giving access to the devil in my life. That's why Paul says, "Bless and do not curse." Why? Is it because cursing or condemning makes me a bad person? No, it's because of what it attracts (Matthew 5:4). Like attracts like. Blessing attracts the kingdom of heaven. Cursing attracts the devil's system or mentality. The Beatitudes are basically the Law of Attraction. Matthew 5:5 says, "Blessed (empowered to prosper) are the meek (humble or submitted to the view and opinion of God)[18] for they shall inherit the earth." By being meek, humble, and submitting to the view and opinion of God, I attract the kingdom of heaven to dominate my environment.

Matthew 3:2 states, "Repent, for the kingdom of heaven is at hand!" (NKJV). This verse is often interpreted to mean, "Have godly sorrow for wrongdoing so that someday you can go to heaven." This is certainly a key element of truth in this verse. However, there is something more here. The term *repent* literally means to think differently or to change your thinking.[19] In other words, change your thinking because you cannot access the kingdom thinking the way you're thinking right now.

It is crucial for us to understand what the kingdom of heaven means in its entirety. The kingdom means *God's rule.* It also means the location and resources of God. The kingdom of God is the governance or system of how to access the kingdom of heaven or God's provision.[20] The declaration of this passage is to change our minds (or thinking) so we can access the resources that God longs to place at our disposal. It is essential that we are operating in the right system—God's kingdom—which is always based on His truth.

God's system (kingdom) operates exactly the opposite of the world's system. In God's system, if you want to receive, you have to give. If you want to increase, you must decrease. If you want to become the greatest, you have to become the least. If you want people to serve you, you must become the servant of all. If you want to live, you have to die. It is vital to gain a new perspective so we can begin to access God's total provisions.

Assuredly, the devil wants to muddle this perception. If I asked you what or who is the number-one enemy to believers, what would you say? Most people would probably respond, "Satan." But satan is already defeated (see Colossians 2:14 -15). Satan's victories come mainly through the realm of influence. Public enemy number one is primarily "the flesh."

What is the flesh? The flesh is not quarreling, anger, or drunkenness. Those are works (or manifestations) of the flesh, which Paul lists in Galatians 5:20-21. According to Romans 8:5-6, the flesh is a mind-set that dictates our actions. It is the root of most bad decisions. According to John 6:63, "the flesh profits nothing" (NKJV). It doesn't take much of a businessman to figure out that you shouldn't invest in something that doesn't produce anything of lasting value.

Paul further tells us that the flesh is the opposite of the Spirit (Galatians 5:16). He even goes on to say "…so that you do not do the things that you wish" (Galatians 5:17, NKJV). You want to access God's system, but you can't, because you're in the wrong system. The world's system promotes the flesh, which puts you in a place contrary to the Spirit. Therefore, you are unable to fully access the kingdom of God. In essence, the flesh is man's feeble attempt to do God's will. Thus, you replace love with lust, or peace with postponement. The problem is this: you tell God not to get involved in your life because you'll take care of it in your own strength. Yet nothing you ever do in the flesh is able to access His provision. It's impossible to manifest His kingdom through the decisions of your flesh.

Now, if the flesh is contrary to the Spirit, the real question is, "What is 'being in the Spirit'?" The idea of *being in the Spirit* means to think of God, to think *like* God, and to think *from* God. When a crisis occurs, you immediately think of God. If you're in the flesh and a conflict arises, instead of thinking according to kingdom principles, you try to figure out what you should do on your own. The sad thing is that so many people don't grasp the futility of self-effort in the flesh! In fact, the Scriptures say that the god of this world has blinded their minds from seeing the truth about Jesus and the kingdom of heaven (see 2 Corinthians 4:4).

To think "like God" means you renew your mind with how God thinks about you and your situation. This means there is no conflict between your spirit and your mind. To think "from God" means you take the time to hear from God. The bottom line of the flesh is you don't think of God, like God, or from God. The flesh becomes man's effort to do God's will. But its very nature negates God fulfilling His will in your life.

That is why Matthew says we need to repent (change the way we think). Only after that change can we access the kingdom of God. You can't access the kingdom thinking the way you're thinking right now. Repentance is more than godly sorrow for wrongdoing; it is changing the core of your thinking to agree with God, which then allows you to tap into the resources of God.

REPENTANCE IS A FIVE-FOLD PROCESS:

Identification—What is the sin, shortcoming, or boundary?

Antidote—What is God's mind-set to break the boundary?

Revelation—Let God's Word become revelation to you to create the proper thinking to break your present limitation. Revelation is something you always knew but never realized. It starts with biblical meditation on the Word of God.

Repetition—Repetition is what solidifies revelation in your personal belief system.

Rethinking—Identification to antidote to revelation to repetition creates rethinking. Rethinking equates to expectancy, which gives way to faith.

Thus, Paul says, "Don't be conformed to this world." The only way to break free from the deception of this world's system is to allow the Word of God to completely transform your thinking.

PRINCIPLE # 2
BE TRANSFORMED

Transformation is the second principle. This term also comes from two words. The prefix, *trans,* means "over, above and beyond, to cross over or to transcend."[21] Once again, *formed* means "way or pattern of doing something." Together this word means thinking over, above, and beyond this world's system. The way you cross over to God's system of provision is by being transformed by His truth.

This term is the Greek word *metamorphose,* which is where we get our English word *metamorphosis.* Metamorphosis at its root means to be radically transformed. When you refer to metamorphosis, you often think of a caterpillar becoming a butterfly. A few hours after it has emerged from its chrysalis, it stretches its wings and leaves the limitations of its former life behind. It is amazing how something that crawls on the ground can transform into a creature of exquisite beauty. That is the kind of total transformation God wants to do in your life. Once you are transformed by His truth, you no longer resemble your former self. You leave one level of living behind and step into the abundant living God has for you.

The secret of God's kingdom is that His provision is limitless, and He did not even spare His own Son so we could have everything (see Romans 8:32).

Someone might come to you and say, "I've seen your life. It doesn't look like much." Your response should be, "Yes, but it is being transformed." Similarly, others might say the same thing about your ministry, church, or even about your spouse. Maybe they say, "I know your husband. He doesn't look like much." Look at them and smile and say, "Yes, but he's being transformed."

Let me illustrate to you what I mean. When my son Jonathan was eleven years old, a relative gave him a gift card to Toys 'R Us. Although he had already spent most of its value, the card had approximately $7.12 left and was burning a hole in his pocket. Jonathan encouraged me to take him shopping. After some persuasion, I agreed to take him to the toy store. As soon as we got inside, he immediately went to the Play Station 2 section. He looked at systems and a number of the games, all of which far exceeded $7.12. I finally convinced him to look at something he could get for the value of his gift card. So we made our way to the action figure area, where he settled on a *Transformer*. If you have never seen these toys, they look like one thing (a person or an animal). By moving a few parts they suddenly transform into something altogether different (a plane, truck, or other vehicle). That is the idea of what Paul is trying to tell us in the opening verses of Romans 12. If you don't conform to the world's system, but are instead transformed, you will be changed into a person who doesn't even resemble your former self. That is why the Bible says you now are a "new creation" (2 Corinthians 5:17).

There is a major difference between being "changed" and being "transformed." On the surface these two terms appear virtually the same, but a careful examination reveals an important difference. The word *change* means "to cause to go from one state to another, to alter, to make different or to cause a difference, to quit one thing and to start another or to substitute."[22]

Transform, on the other hand, suggests "to alter form or appearance, a metamorphosis, to conform to the will of God, a release of Divine nature, an alteration of the heart, to change in inner nature, to change one's mind or to exchange."[23]

As you can see, change is something that comes from the outside in, while transformation comes from the inside out. Transformation is an inward effortless alteration. The problem with much of Christianity is that we have tried to change the outside through behavior modification. No wonder so many people begin to question whether real change can happen for them. We must show them that true transformation brings alteration from the inside out through the power of Christ's life within us. The question becomes how?

PRINCIPLE # 3
RENEW YOUR MIND

That leads us to the third principle, *renewing your mind.* Transformation comes by the renewing of the mind. *Renew* is another fascinating word. It means "to renovate or to restore to its original state."[24] If you renovate something, you take out old things and put in new things. Recently, we renovated our café at our Bible school. We took out old ceiling tiles and put in new ones. We took out old flooring and put in new high gloss tile. We recovered old tables with "retro" tops. We got rid of everything that was old and replaced it with brand-new things.

The same holds true for our lives. If you don't like the output (manifestation), you have to change the input. We understand this in computer language: "Garbage in, garbage out." We often can quote the right formula, but if we don't like the output, most of the time we keep focusing on the output. There is a success law called the Law of Correspondence, which states that your outer world is in direct correspondence to your inner world.[25] If you want to change your output, you must change your input.

To achieve a new level of living, you have to get rid of your old ways of thinking and replace them with new thoughts. Once new dominant thoughts take root in your heart, they will bring about new actions that result in new manifestations. Proverbs 23:7 tells us, "[As a man] thinks in his heart so is he," (NKJV). The term *think* used here means "door-keeper or gatekeeper."[26] In other words, dominant thoughts are the gate-keeper to your heart. What gets in your heart is what you are going to do. It does not mean it will maybe, possibly, or probably happen—it *will* happen. You will do whatever is in your heart.

Proverbs 4:23 amplifies on this important truth: "Keep your heart will all diligence, for out of it spring the issues of life" (NKJV). There are several things that are essential here:

"Above all else" means the highest priority of your life is to guard your heart, for out of it will come the manifestations of your life.

Guard your heart, for out of it come the "issues" of life. This term, *issues,* means "boundaries, limitations, or stagnations."[27] Your boundaries in life are not the product of your background, education, or race (by themselves). They are not about what your mother or father said, or what your friends did. Your boundaries are about one thing…what is in your heart. If you want to change your manifestations, limitations, or boundaries, you must change your heart.

The question is, how is that done? Most of us say things when we don't truly know what they mean. We say, "You've got to believe from your heart," or "Do it from your heart." What does that mean? How do I do that?

The Bible says in Hebrews 4:12 that "the word of God is living and active (NIV), sharper than any two-edged sword, piercing even to the dividing asunder of soul and spirit, and of the joints and marrow, and is a discerner of the thoughts and intents of the heart" (KJV). This verse is primarily about the Word of God, but it also gives great insight into the heart. Hebrews tells us that the Word of God is alive, constantly active and full of energy to carry out the intent of the will of God.[28] The Word is "sharper than a two-edged sword." There is a reason why the author used this term. The common weapon of that era was a one-edged sword. The Roman Empire had just pioneered a two-edged sword, a sword that cut both ways. This innovation turned the Roman armies into the most powerful force on earth. The writer is using an analogy to show us that the Word of God is more powerful than any existing weapon and is full of energy to fulfill the will of God for your life.

The purpose of this sword (Word) is to pierce the heart[29] and to "divide asunder" the aspects of the heart. The term, *divide asunder,* means to separate for the purpose of distinction. The question becomes, what is it distinguishing? What is the heart?

Hebrews tells us what the heart is:

There are two aspects of the heart that the Word penetrates and separates; the soul and the spirit.[30] The job of the heart is to mediate the soul by the spirit. When these two aspects line up, nothing is impossible with God.

Your spirit is the place where God dwells, where He speaks to you (Romans 8:10, 16). The soul is your mind, will, emotions, and imagination.[31] Your spirit man is a new creation and is perfect (2 Corinthians 5:17; Hebrews 12:23). The soul, however, has to be renewed with God's truth. That is the only way you will be able to make His promises work in your life. Therefore, the job of your heart is to line up the soul with

The Heart

Soul   Spirit

Joint   Marrow

Thought   Intents

MIND / **CONSCIOUS**   **CONSCIENCE**
WILL   **SUB-CONSCIOUS**   **MORAL VALUE**
EMOTIONS   **SYSTEM**
IMAGINATION

the Spirit. When these two forces are in agreement, then the energy and power of God are released in people. The Word divides and discerns the thoughts and intents of the heart. Thoughts precede actions, and intents (moral understanding or conscience)[32] precede thoughts. God made man to operate out of his spirit, but he is often sabotaged by a soul not aligned with its intent.

The problem is that most people operate out of their soul rather than their spirit. Often an event or set of circumstances you encounter will affect you emotionally. According to research, emotions travel 80,000 times faster than thoughts.[33] That is why we are most often affected by our emotions rather than principles. In turn, your emotions affect your will, your will affects your mind, and your mind affects your actions. If we do not line up our lives by kingdom principles, then our un-renewed soul will wreak havoc in our lives. (Of course, the opposite is true as well. If renewed truth encounters us emotionally, it too affects us in our will, mind, and actions. The result is positive change.)

Your mind is also made up of two aspects: the conscious and the subconscious. The job of the conscious mind is to analyze new information, compare it with current information, and determine truth in your life. The subconscious mind is like a huge data bank that records every thought, idea, emotion, or experience. It doesn't reason. Its job is to make come to pass what your conscious mind determines is true. It will work to make sure your words and actions stay in line with your self-image. This part of your mind creates habits, comfort zones, and consistency. (In this way, you don't have to learn things over and over.) It creates an automatic response system and is where your personal belief system exists. Psychologists suggest that 90 to 95 percent of your daily decisions come out of your subconscious mind.

The repercussions and effects of this are obvious. As long as your conscious mind tells the subconscious mind truth that is healthy and productive, this is an incredible system. If, however, through experiences and improper training the conscious mind has adopted "beliefs" that are contrary to the Word of God, it will produce wrong responses and actions that limit us and prevent us from growing in corresponding areas. Though we have an unlimited Gospel, many of us are leading a limited life because of our un-renewed minds.

Let me give you an example of how these two aspects of the mind work. If I taught you how to drive a car, you would first learn to drive at a conscious level. Everything would be very mechanical. You would slowly learn all the mechanics—the steering wheel, brake, accelerator, speedometer, etc. Once this process becomes a learned procedure (habit) by going from the conscious level to a subconscious level, you lose the discomfort of the rote mechanical process. In fact, many people can drive while listening to the radio, having a conversation, and talking on a cell phone all at the same time. You are able to do all of this without even thinking about it. The subconscious mind has created a habit and a comfort zone.

In most areas of your life the subconscious mind creates habits, personal belief systems, and comfort zones. The job of the subconscious mind is to create consistency. So, it strives to keep you in that comfort zone, so much so that if you violate it without new programming, it will work to keep you there even if it has to sabotage you.

It is what some psychologists call a "set-point"—a mind-set or a self-limiting belief. This would be similar to flying an airplane and setting the automatic pilot at 30,000 feet; the airplane would maintain that altitude. If I grabbed the controls and ascended to 35,000 feet or descended to 20,000 feet, once I released the controls the plane would return to 30,000 feet.

That is exactly how the subconscious mind works. Its job is to create habits that keep you consistent. If those habits are productive and beneficial, that becomes a real benefit. However, if your habits and beliefs are unproductive or destructive, they place limitations on your life. Your subconscious mind must be renewed to the truth in order to break "set-points," those self-limiting beliefs that prevent you from experiencing what God has provided for you.

This is the reason why so many studies reveal that 80 percent of lottery winners who win millions of dollars end up back where they started after a short period of time. It is why so many people "yoyo" diet. Around 95 percent of people who lose weight on diets return to their original weight. You don't see things as they are; you see things as you are. Your subconscious mind will try to keep you aligned with how your self-image perceives itself. It is also one of the key reasons why pastors or sales representatives can't break certain number barriers. The subconscious mind will actually work to keep you at the same comfort zone or sabotage your efforts unless the mind is renewed. Your thinking at the subconscious level creates comfort zones that ultimately affect your destiny.

A classic example in history illustrates this point. In 1953 no runner had ever broken the four-minute mile barrier. In fact, many thought it was impossible. Some physicians and trainers of the era even believed it could not be accomplished without damaging a person's heart and possibly resulting in death. Despite the prevalent mind-set of the day, one man in England, Roger Bannister, believed it could be done. He put himself through rigorous mental and physical training. In 1954 he became the first man to break the four-minute barrier. The impossible became possible.

Here is what's really amazing about the feat. Once Bannister did it, someone else broke his record within one month. Before the end of the year, six others broke the four-minute mile. Within another year, sixty people had broken the barrier. When people thought it was impossible, it was impossible. When a man believed in his heart, and changed his thinking, what was considered to be impossible became possible.

PRINCIPLE # 4
PROVE THE WILL OF GOD

Romans 12:2 admonishes us in the fourth principle to "prove what is the good, acceptable and perfect will of God." The term *prove* means "to establish as genuine, approve, validate, discern or to recognize, revelation or by implication to manifest."[34]

Once you are no longer conformed to this world's system (breaking free from its limitations), but instead are transformed to a higher way of thinking (by renewing your mind and establishing your heart), you will be able to recognize, validate, and manifest God's will for your life. It's time to think differently and live life the way God intended.

Renewed thinking and a transformed heart result in a recognition of heaven's resources and open the doors to God's kingdom. During a meeting with Oral Roberts one day, he told me that miracles are coming to us all the time. People either receive them, or they pass by them. It is really a matter of whether people recognize them or not.

In your brain there is something that causes you to filter out unimportant information and focus on meaningful facts or opportunities. It is called the Reticular Activating System. There are three aspects to RAS:

Positive Focusing—One example of positive focusing is when a party is taking place in a noisy room, and down the hallway comes the faint cry of a baby. No one hears the baby except the mother. Why? Because she is focused on her baby.

Negative Filtering—An example of this is a person who has a home close to the airport. You may wonder how they could sleep in a house with planes flying over every few minutes. The occupants of this home have no trouble because they have filtered the noise out of their thinking.

Individual Perception—This occurs when two people see the same accident but give two totally different accounts. Why? They each had a different vantage point or perception of what happened.

RAS causes you to filter unimportant information and focus on what is important for the moment. It immediately transmits vital information into your consciousness. It causes us to recognize things we might otherwise miss.

The key factor to these four renewal principles (keys) is this: Once you follow them, you will begin to see things from a different perspective. If you are not conformed to this world's system, then you filter out its system and you focus in on God's system. When your mind is transformed and your heart is established (your soul and spirit are lined up to truth), you will be able to perceive and receive the provision of God's limitless kingdom, which is now at your disposal. The Holy Spirit will bring to you people, ideas, and resources according to your most dominant thoughts. A renewed mind recognizes them and finds a way to bring them to pass.

This is the dominant law in the kingdom. We attract to ourselves according to our dominant images and renewed thinking. You will invariably attract from God people, ideas, and resources that line up with His kingdom.

You become like a human magnet. A person renewed to kingdom thinking attracts the provision of the kingdom of heaven unto himself. For example, atoms under a microscope possess a magnetic field, but they are discharged. The atoms of a nail all point in various directions and, thus, cancel out one another's electromagnetic charge. By contrast, if they are aligned or congruent, that is north and south point in the same direction, then the magnet will attract a nail.[35] People who are congruent (line up with God's truth and kingdom principles) are magnetic. They attract to themselves according to their most dominant thoughts.

In Mark Victor Hanson's book *The One Minute Millionaire,* he gives three principles to congruency: (1) Desire, (2) Belief, and (3) Self-image.[36] All three of these are found in Mark 11:24: "Therefore, I say unto you, whatever things you ask when you pray, *believe* that you receive them and you will have them" (NKJV).

THE THREE LAWS TO CONGRUENCY

1. **Desire**—The term *desire* here means "craving enough to sacrifice for."[37] The idea is not just something you want. What are you willing to sacrifice for? You may have to read a book to increase knowledge. You might want to go to a seminar, get a tape series to listen to, go to night school, etc. Put yourself in a position of expertise by desiring it with all your heart. Go after it with passion.

2. **Believe**—This means you transform your personal belief system until you feel it. (Feelings in a circumstance will reveal what you believe.) Establishing a belief system in accordance with God's kingdom is essential and must be intentional. Beliefs don't just happen; they are cultivated by focusing on what is true.

3. **Self-image**—You can never rise above the image you have of yourself in your heart. If you want to change an area in your life, you must change your heart's view of yourself.

This then is the "believe" Jesus is talking about in Mark 11:24. This is accessing heaven's provision for your life. The problem for most people is that they are dominated in their thinking by what they don't want. Your subconscious mind can't tell the difference between real or imagined or positive and negative.[38] It just recognizes dominant thoughts and acts on them. Then it concentrates its efforts to make those things come to pass. The subconscious mind is impersonal. It acts according to bad or good, according to what you've told it. It simply manifests what you are thinking. So, when people use dominant thoughts like "I can't handle the work load," "There's not enough time," "I can't afford this," "I don't have the ability," "Nobody wants to hear me," "I don't want debt," your subconscious mind begins to work to make the dominant thoughts come to pass. Thus, the Law of Attraction is working whether you believe it or not. That's why Henry Ford said, "Whether you think you can or you can't, either way you're right."

Galatians 6:7-8 says, "God cannot be mocked. A man reaps what he sows. The one who sows to please his sinful nature, from that nature will reap destruction; the one who sows to please the Spirit, from the Spirit will reap eternal life" (*zoe,* in Greek means the God kind of life). The reason God is not mocked is because you reap or attract what you sow. If you have dominant thoughts of "I can't," it is what you will manifest. If you have thoughts of "I can," your renewed mind will find a way to make it come to pass.

The Law of Attraction is really little more than Oral Roberts' "seed faith" on steroids. The Law of Attraction is sowing and reaping, combined with renewing the mind.

"Seed faith" has three basic tenets, based on Galatians 6:7:

Seed faith says, *"God is my source."* The Law of Attraction says: "The kingdom of heaven has your provision."

Seed faith says, *"Give and it shall be given unto you."* The Law of Attraction says, "Renew your mind, and as you obey Kingdom law you attract God's provision." Obedience to kingdom law initiates and authorizes heavenly provision on your behalf.

Seed faith says, *"Expect a Miracle."* The Law of Attraction says, "You attract, anticipate, and receive God's blessings."

In my early days at Oral Roberts University, Oral Roberts would talk about *seed faith.* It wasn't primarily about prosperity. He would say, "If you want a friend, be a friend. If you need someone to help you, help someone else. If you want God to bless you, be a blessing to others. It is giving and receiving; sowing and reaping. It is Joshua 1:8, "Don't let this book of the Law depart out of your mouth. Meditate therein day and night. Then I will make you prosperous and you will have good success."

Now, let's turn our attention to "Attraction Action." How do I apply mind renewal to attract the kingdom of heaven to my life practically?

KEYS

"God's Extreme Makeover" comes from the inside out. Your outside world directly correlates to your inside world.

All laws of success and productivity culminate at the Law of Attraction.

"Learned helplessness" or "strongholds" in 2 Corinthians 10:4 is when you feel powerless to change things, even if it is contrary to the will of God.

There are four "keys" to create a renewed mind and a new personal belief system in Romans 12:2:

1. Don't be conformed to the world's system.
2. Be transformed (to a higher system).
3. ...by the renewing of the mind.
4. Prove or manifest the will of God.

Chapter 3

PRODUCTIVITY THEOLOGY:
Attraction Action

THE *LAW OF ATTRACTION* SAYS "like attracts like." Transforming your personal belief system is how we activate a positive attraction action. Often we've limited ourselves by what we think is possible. Positive attraction is demonstrated in the amazing story of Cliff Young. In 1983 Cliff Young set a new world record for the six hundred km race in his native country of Australia. He not only broke the world record, he shattered it by thirty-six hours. What makes this feat even more amazing is that he was sixty-one years old when he did it. And Cliff Young was not a world-class athlete. He was a local farmer who didn't realize he was doing what was impossible.

All trained athletes who run this long-distance ultra-marathon know the proper strategy. You run eighteen hours and then rest six hours. You run those intervals like clockwork until you complete the race, going from race to restoration to race. The only problem was no one told that to Cliff Young. He thought you were supposed to run the race straight through. Unwittingly, he ran the race straight through and demolished the world record.

We are only limited by what we think is possible. It's the old adage of the bumble bee, who doesn't know his wings are too small to allow him to fly. But he flies anyway. Most of our limitations are self-imposed. When we learn to remove those limitations by learning who we truly are in Christ, we'll soar to new heights in every area of our lives. We've already seen the four foundational kingdom principles that will give us a renewed mind, an established heart, and a transformed personal belief system in order to accomplish this:

1. Do not be conformed to the world's system,

2. but be transformed (to the Kingdom of God),

3. by renewing your mind,

4. and prove (recognize and seize) the will of God.

These key principles form a pattern that helps establish a new identity in people. Second Corinthians 5:17 states, "Therefore, if anyone is in Christ, he is a new creation; the old has gone, the new has come!" This verse shows the key difference between the Old Covenant and the New Covenant. It isn't about people trying to live for God, but living through Christ (Galatians 2:20), who now indwells you by His Holy Spirit. This personal encounter with God gives people a new spirit, a new nature, and a new identity. Once you are born again, God creates a new nature in you. You now have new inherent tendencies, new instincts, and an inborn character that comes from God. Your spirit is brand new, but your mind has to be renewed.

You are not a person with two natures; you have been given a new one (Romans 6:6). The problem with most believers is that after they become a new creation, they tend to operate out of their old identity. They don't see themselves as a new person. When the Bible talks about an "old nature" or "carnal nature," it is referring to what has been crucified with Christ. The exhortation of Scripture is to no longer think in terms of that old nature, but to see yourself in the new identity (new creation) God has now given you (see Ephesians 4:20-24; Colossians 3:10).

The "carnal nature" (see Romans 8:5; Galatians 5:16) is nothing more than the *flesh*. The *flesh* is a mind-set that dictates what action we will or will not take (see Romans 8:5-8). The *flesh* is man's futile attempt to try to do God's will in his own strength. Lust is a perverted substitute for love and sensitivity (see Ephesians 4:17-19). Greed is a selfish substitute for true prosperity. The only reason a person sins is to meet a need in their lives.[1] The declaration of 2 Corinthians 5:17 is to liberate you from your old identity and to focus in on the new nature God has placed in you. It is a recognition of the new person you became when you invited Jesus into your heart to become your Savior and Lord. God wants you to recognize the transformation of your life as a new creature and begin operating in your newfound identity. In other words, you can't change your condition until you change your position (your understanding of who you are in Christ).

Your spirit man is completely brand new, but your mind must be renewed to kingdom principles so you can operate in your full potential as a person. In other words, your new heart (Ezekiel 36:26, 27) has one primary function: to mediate your soul by your spirit (Hebrews 4:12). Once you clearly recognize your new identity, you won't try to operate out of your old nature, and God will begin to manifest His will for your life. This is precisely what Scripture means when it talks about crucifying the flesh or dying to self (Romans 6:6, 8; Galatians 2:20; Romans 8:13; Ephesians 4:23-24). The scientific meaning of *death,* according to one source, means "to fall out of correspondence with."[2] When I die to self, I fall out of correspondence with my old identity and now recognize who God made me to be. I no longer see life through my old perspective. My new nature gives me a new "image" of life. This single perspective will do more to change a person and allow them to see God's will than almost anything I know.

What is the good, acceptable, and perfect will of God for you (Romans 12:2 NKJV)? Jesus' statement in John 10:10 is God's will for you. "The thief (devil) comes only to steal and kill and destroy…." You might want to rejoice that the verse doesn't end there. It goes on to say, "…I (Jesus) came that they might have life, and have it abundantly" (NASB). This term *abundance* means "superabundance in quantity, superior in quality, excess, surplus, excel, superfluous or extreme."[3] God's will for you is abundance.

God's will for you is further elaborated in an amazing statement in Ephesians 3:20: "Now to Him who is able to do exceedingly, abundantly above all that we ask or think ("imagine" in NIV) according to the power that works in us." Able to do what? He is able to prosper you, heal you, help you, love you, grant you joy, and cause you to succeed at every level. But beyond the fact He is able, He is willing "to do" it. How conflicting would it be for a heavenly Father to be able to do something, but then not do it. He's not only able, but He's going to do it if we'll learn about the new power He has placed in us.

He is able to do "exceedingly." This term *exceedingly* means "to exceed, go beyond, take the limits off, limitless, excessive, too much (exhaustless and then some on top of that)."[4] Our God is not God of just enough, but He is God of too much. He is El Shaddai (the God of more than enough), not "El Cheapo."

He does all this "according to the power at work within us." We don't simply work for God, but we work through Him. When He came to live in us, He deposited all the power of the Godhead bodily (see Colossians 2:9) in us. We now have this new nature that wants to release power so we can do things in excess and in the extreme. The problem is we still identify and operate out of who we used to be. Our focus is wrong. For many people, the idea of a God who is excessive, extreme, or too much is beyond their thinking (set-point). If you've ever been around someone who has come out of the financial disaster of the Great Depression, listen to how they speak. They're always saying things like "that is enough," or "that's good enough." The reason is they have been conditioned to think in terms of limitation because of the scarcity they had to face during that time. It is difficult for them to relate to a God who is more than enough or extreme.

One time I did a meeting in a small community near Omaha, Nebraska. The congregation was not a particularly big setting on Sunday morning. We started out with about 225 people. By the time of the last night of the meetings, on Tuesday, the services had grown by about 100 people. About 90 of the 100 new people were young people who came from the local high school. These students were so excited about what they were receiving, they went and got their friends and brought them to the meetings.

On the final night of this series of meetings, I gave an altar call. As I looked down at the altar, this is what I saw: to my right were bikers with head bands, leather coats cut off at the sleeves, tattoos, and chains. In the middle were guys with green, yellow, and purple hair. To my right were satanists. That is what you call a sight to behold. I looked down in awe at this proportionately large group of people, wondering what I should do next. Lovingly, the Holy Spirit said to me, "Pray for them." So I began to pray that God would break into their lives in a radical way.

As I worked my way around the altar to where this satanist was, it didn't take real discernment to tell she had a serious problem. It was obvious she had some deep emotional and spiritual needs. Her hair was cut short and dyed a deep black. She had on white pancake makeup, and her eyeliner and lipstick were also deep black. By all outward appearances she looked deeply troubled.

Earlier in the week a young man had been delivered and saved out of satanism, and now he had brought some of his satanist friends to the meeting. I walked up to this young woman and gently asked her if she was ready to give her heart to Christ. She just stared at me defiantly.

Suddenly, I was moved by the Spirit, and I gently said to her, "You're not ready. Go sit back down." You could almost hear a gasp come out of the pastoral staff. I knew what they must have been thinking, "You have an opportunity to have a satanist at the altar, and you tell her to go sit down? What's wrong with you?"

As I continued to minister to people, I watched this young man who had been saved earlier in the week. He went over and grabbed his friend by the collar and dragged her back down to the altar. I came over to her a second time, and I gently asked her again, "Are you ready to give your heart to Christ?" Again, she defiantly stared at me, and a second time I said, "You don't know who you are. Go sit down." Now, these pastors were ready to pick up stones and stone me.

As I was finishing my ministry at the altar, about five or ten minutes later I saw this young man once again grab her by the collar and drag her to the altar a third time. I walked up to her a third time and asked, "Are you ready to give your heart to Christ?"

This time huge tears started running down her cheeks. All that white and black makeup got all mixed together. She looked like someone out of the rock group "KISS." I then had the marvelous opportunity to lead her in a prayer for her salvation. Afterward, I laid hands on her, and she received a dramatic deliverance from her past bondages to satanism. As I was leaving the auditorium through the lobby after the meeting, I saw her standing across the area. I went over to her and asked if I could ask her a question. In her new demeanor she agreed. I looked at her and asked, "What was it that finally caused you to give your life to Christ?"

She looked at me with new wide-eyed enthusiasm and said, "I finally met someone and something that was more extreme than I was." People in this world are looking for people who live life and live it to the extreme.

KEYS TO A RENEWED MIND

The real question is, "How do I renew my mind and establish my heart in accordance to these four transforming principles found in Romans 12:2?" Remember, it is something that has to be intentional on your part. It will not happen automatically. By learning to set your intention we can target growth and productivity on purpose. The scientific community has made some amazing discoveries of how to target change. The good news is, there's not only a prescribed way to do it, but they've also discovered the time table it takes to accomplish it.

Dr. Maxwell Maltz, in the 1960s, was a very successful reconstructive and cosmetic facial surgeon. Though he had given his patients the perfect faces they wanted, he noticed that many of them still suffered from deep personal scars of insecurity on the inside. He discovered that changing the outside of a person doesn't always provide the transformation they truly desire. Maltz eventually decided to move from treating "outer scars" to trying to heal "inner scars" in the people on which he had operated. He went on to become the father of something called Psycho-Cybernetics, a system of thought for self-improvement. He believed that people had distorted perceptions of themselves because of wrong beliefs in their subconscious mind, so he sought to help them with his new philosophy.

During his medical studies on people who had undergone amputation, Maltz learned an interesting fact about behavioral modification. He discovered that a person who lost a limb "experienced" a phantom limb for around three weeks after the operation. In other words, even though the limb was gone, the person felt as if they still possessed the limb and would often try to use it for about three weeks. The conclusion was, it takes about three weeks to change thoughts.

Maltz applied the same theory to behavioral change and reached similar conclusions. It takes twenty-one days to create a new habit. No matter where you are in life, you can change the course of your life in three weeks.

Now, here is a central key to transforming your life: ideas and actions contrary to a person's core value system (spirit) will not be accepted or acted upon if they are contrary to a person's personal belief system (soul). Proverbs 4:23 tells us about how our boundaries are established: Above all else, guard your heart, for it is the wellspring (for out of it spring the issues, NKJV) ("boundary" in Hebrews) of life."

I may say to you, "Prayer will change your life. Prayer will change your church. Prayer will change your city." You may nod your head in agreement with what you know to be true on the surface, but in your personal belief system, you prayed for someone once and they died, or you didn't get the result you anticipated. Chances are you aren't praying consistently.

A similar example might be prosperity. Someone may say to you, "Give and you shall receive" (Luke 6:38). The Laws of Reciprocity and Attraction state, "As a man sows, shall he also reap" (Galatians 6:7). But in your personal belief system, you see giving as a depletion of your resources, or you think you know someone who gives, but they are still struggling. The chances are that you will not be a person who tithes, even though the Scripture plainly says that God will open the windows of heaven (Malachi 3:10) in reference to your giving.

God has given you an innate ability to create and be productive (see earlier definition of "image," chapter 2). The real question comes down to how do you make the renewing of the mind process applicable so that you can attract the kingdom to yourself? How do I create new thoughts and habits for productivity?

The on-going problem is that you are giving mental ascent to truth that is contrary to what you really believe in your heart. Similarly, people try to break limitations off their lives, but they fall back into old mindsets because of certain set-points in their thinking. Psychologist Sigmund Freud writes on what he called "The Pain/Pleasure Principle."[5] His assertion was that people will always make decisions based on what they see as pleasure and avoid what they see as pain. Let's use pornography as an example. If a person views pornography as pleasure and God stopping him as pain, it will be virtually impossible to break the habit with any permanence. If, however, he sees God's blessing as pleasure and pornography as pain keeping him from the blessing, breaking the habit would be much easier. The Pain/Pleasure Principle affects a person's personal belief system and the time that it takes to change habits.

Most people are predisposed to make excuses for their shortcomings. George Washington Carver once said, "99 percent of all failure comes from people who have a habit of making excuses." The moment we begin to blame someone or something else, we unwittingly dis-empower ourselves from being able to conquer our boundaries.

Earl Nightengale said, "Study anything for 1 hour per day for 5 years and you will become an expert on that topic."

In other words, you don't have to settle for your present limitation; you can break your present barriers.

4 APPLICATIONS TO 4 PRINCIPLES

How to apply the Romans 12:2 principles:

Be not conformed to the world's system, but

be transformed

by the renewing of your mind

so that you can prove the will of God.

Here are the *4 C's in the application:*

1. The first application is *cognitive dissonance:* This is a fancy psychological word that simply means mental discord. The first step to changing our personal belief system is to understand the source of our thinking. Our homes, our schools, our parents, our teachers, our churches, our friends, etc., have all helped create mind-sets (set-points) and expectations in our lives. Once a very "significant other" in my life told me, "You will never amount to anything." I thought to myself, *If this person loved me and this is*

what they saw, it must be true. Invariably, every time I got ready to break through to a new level in my life, I would sabotage myself and remain at the same level. In the deepest part of my being, my subconscious mind believed I wouldn't amount to anything. Many people can't break certain limitations because of similar cognitive dissonance they have experienced in life. It wasn't until I renewed my mind to my new identity in Christ, that I was able to break-through to a new level in my life.

James Allen, the author of *As a Man Thinketh,* says, "A plan consistently, persistently adhered to, good or bad, in abundance or scarcity, will produce results in a person's life." It is Proverbs 4:23 bringing the "issues" (boundaries) to fruition.

Cognitive Dissonance simply means "duality or duplicity in a person's thinking." It is what we find explained in James 1:6-8, "But when he asks, he must believe and not doubt, because he who doubts is like a wave of the sea, blown and tossed by the wind. That man should not think he will receive anything from the Lord; he is a double-minded man, unstable in all he does."

The term used for "double-minded" here means "double souled."[6] In other words, your mind, will, emotions, and imagination are vacillating in opinion or purpose and creating doubt. Your soul is vacillating in opinion from what your spirit is saying and creating a divided heart (Hosea 10:2). The result is an unstable person, fluctuating or incongruent, in his ways or his willingness to do something. A divided heart causes a person to either sabotage his own efforts or it creates an apprehension to step out and try. When core values and personal beliefs are in conflict, it creates immobilization at best, and a person remains fixed in their present state.

How does a person overcome cognitive dissonance? Psychologists encourage *Cognitive Restructuring* in order to stop "double-mindedness." *Cognitive Restructuring* has two steps:

Step 1 is ***emotional implantation.*** Emotional implantation is when someone or something "yanks your chain," and suddenly you realize you don't have to be this way anymore. Let me give you an example of this principle. Everyone knows the story of Ebenezer Scrooge. What caused Scrooge to go from miser to philanthropist overnight? The answer is simple. He saw the Ghosts of Christmas Past, Present, and Future. He had an emotional implantation. Suddenly, he realized the course of his life was heading the wrong way, and he saw the need to change before it was too late.

For us as believers, this means we have a divine encounter with God or a revelation of His truth that alters our perception. Sometimes it is a special touch from God as we are praying and reading His Word. It's our repent (a change in thinking) experience. Unfortunately, most of us leave it there. We miss the critical second step.

Step 2 is ***repetition***. You simply rehearse your new thought or identity over and over again, until you create a new habit or thought process. How long does this take? According to Maxwell Maltz, it takes 21 days. Some psychologists say it takes 30 days, and others say 42 or even 60 days. The Pain/Pleasure Principle can affect the length of time of the change, but change can be targeted and brought to resolve in a fairly short period of time.

The real key is this: you don't see things as *they* are; you see things as *you* are in your heart. If you have a wrong image of yourself, it colors the way you see life. We'll discuss this further in the next chapter. F. F. Bosworth once said, "It is impossible to claim by faith what you don't know is the will of God." Faith begins where the will of God is known (in the heart).

2. The second application is ***confession.*** Joshua 1:8 says, "Do not let this Book of the Law depart from your mouth; meditate on it day and night, so that you may be careful to do everything written in it. Then you will be prosperous and successful." ("good success" KJV). The next three principles come out of this verse. "Do not let this Book of the Law depart from your mouth…." Let the Word continuously be on your lips…confess it, continually. There's been much written about confession in the last twenty years. It is similar to what psychologists call "self-talk." Some psychologists even suggest 95 percent of your emotions are determined by the way you talk to yourself.[7] Several years ago, I had the privilege of listening, via tape, to Lou Tice of the Pacific Institute. On a tape concerning "self-talk," he referred to the study of psycholinguistics. He said it was not only important to confess something, but how you confess it makes all the difference in the world. He said, "If you simply confess something, it goes into your personal belief system (PBS) about 10 percent. If you confess it with imagination, your PBS retains about 55 percent. If you confess with imagination and emotion, it will go into your personal belief system 100 percent."

Here is what this means. Confession or declaring the truth of God's Word alone won't by itself transform your personal belief system. Along with confession you need imagination. Imagination is the ability to see without limitation (Ephesians 3:20). It is a form of biblical meditation that allows you to see yourself according to the truth and to intentionally increase your faith. In other words, see yourself in your mind in a way that is commensurate or aligned with His truth. When done repeatedly, this allows the conscious mind to give the subconscious mind new truth. Then, your subconscious mind can work with the Holy Spirit to make it come to pass. Lastly, do it with emotion. How do you do that? Two ways: (1) Use emotional words. Here is an example: "I am excited about (or enjoy, love) making (an amount of money) per year." Your goal should be increase, and that goal should be within what is real for you. Remember, an emotion travels 80,000 times faster than a thought. Feelings empower you to the fact that the truth in you is possible. (2) Allow yourself to have the feelings you would experience if your goal was already realized. This reinforces your subconscious mind to think of itself aligned to your goal.

There is a second set of principles that govern confession. Some psychologists and motivators who promote "confession" contend that this practice should also be linked to the 3 P's:

1. Personal

2. Positive

3. Present tense[9]

Make it personal by using "I." Make it positive. Never focus on the problem, but focus on the solution. Whatever your dominant thoughts are is what you will attract. Thinking about debt, for instance, attracts debt. For example, "I'm not going to eat as much" is focused on the problem and the future. Instead, say, "I'm excited about feeling fit and healthy at (whatever) weight." Also make it present tense, for God lives in the eternal now. Thus, all confessions should begin with "I am."

Confess the truth of God's Word, picture yourself according to the truth, and say and feel the emotion of this event as a finished reality. This is calling the things that are not as though they were (Romans 4:17).

This is why Romans 10 talks about confessing with your mouth and believing with your heart. Ancient Hebrews believed that by memorizing Scripture and confessing with your mouth, the Word went from your head to your heart. Listen to these verses: "But what does it say? "The word is near you; it is in your mouth and in your heart; that is the word of faith we are proclaiming: That if you confess with your mouth, and believe in your heart, you will be saved" (NKJV). For it is with the heart that you believe and are justified, and it is with your mouth you confess and are saved (*Sodzo* means "save, deliver, protect, heal, preserve, do well, make whole, rescue.")[10] Your mouth affects your heart, and in turn, your heart affects your mouth. Matthew 12:34 states, "…for out of the abundance of the heart the mouth speaks" (NKJV). Verse 35 even goes on to say, "The good man brings good things (good manifested) out of the good stored up in him and the evil man brings evil things (done) out of the evil stored up in him."

We store things in our heart by meditation (Psalms 1:1-2; 4:20-23; 37:4; Joshua 1:8) and confession (Joshua 1:8; Romans 10:8, 10; Matthew 12:34, 35). What is in our heart can be discerned by what comes out of our mouth. This affects what we believe, feel, and do. Ultimately, this will bring the manifestation of good success.

3. The third application is ***consistency.*** Repetition is the key to all learning. Repetition (consistency) is the vehicle by which the subconscious mind (SCM) sees a new image of you. You think a thing repeatedly until truth casts a new image in you.

4. Lastly, the fourth application is ***conation.*** Conation is a psychology term that means "to make an effort or to pursue a thing or to

act on what is known."[11] A friend of mine who studied this term told me at its root it means, "You can't stop me unless you kill me."[12] In other words, you must put some resolve into pursuing your dreams. If you are going to do something, then do it with "passion of desire." Later, we will talk about what the Bible means by "desire." Suffice it to say for now, according to Mark 11:22-24, the term *desire* means "wanting something for which you are willing to sacrifice."[13] A strong desire allows you to stand your ground until your personal belief system is established. This is what we see in Matthew 11:12, "From the days of John the Baptist until now the kingdom has been forcefully advancing, and forceful men lay hold of it."

Let me finish this amazing set of principles by giving an illustration from personal experience. Early in my ministry, I had a leader in my church who had unsuccessfully tried to lead a local judge to the Lord. In frustration, he came to me and asked if I would visit his friend and share the Gospel. I agreed to do it, and later that day I left my pastoral office and got into my little pastoral car, took a little pastoral trip to this judge's house, to do my pastoral duty. When I arrived at the judge's house, it was a beautiful spring day. The door was open, but a screen door shielded the entry. I knocked, and a hospice worker greeted me, let me in, and then walked me down the corridor to his bedroom. What awaited me shocked my "pastoral" sense of duty out of me, as I came face to face with grim reality.

I had heard much about Judge Lee. I knew he was a big man, but what I witnessed as I entered his bedroom was a jolt into reality as I witnessed a failing shell of humanity. His frail skeletal frame revealed a dying man.

Seeing his grim condition rocked me to the core of my being and stirred a deep-seated compassion in my heart. I knew I had to share the life of Jesus with this man, but I also realized I had no connection with him, no bridge to share the Gospel. So I asked this prestigious judge what he most liked in life. His answer was fishing. In all honesty, I hate fishing, but the next hour was consumed with talk of rods, lures, lines, bait, etc.

After that hour, we seemed to have a real connection. I looked at him and asked him if he had ever made Jesus the Savior and Lord of his life. He looked at me and assured me he was a good Baptist, but he had never made a personal decision for Christ. I led him in a prayer of salvation. At the conclusion of the prayer, I shared some meaning to his experience and exchanged some more pleasantries. As I got up to leave, the Holy Spirit stopped me dead in my tracks and said, "Tell the man he can be healed!"

I mockingly said to myself, *But he doesn't believe in that sort of thing.* It was like I was expecting God to say, "Oh, I'm sorry, here I stopped you on the way out of the door and everything."

In the midst of my conviction, I turned to him and said, "Do you know you can be healed?"

"I've never heard of such a thing," he replied.

I told him I had a six-part series on faith I had just completed. I suggested that he listen to one tape per day until I visited him again about this time next week.

When I arrived again the next week, it was the same scenario. It was a beautiful spring day, and I was once again greeted by a hospice worker who escorted me to his room. The scenario looked the very same. It was the same disease, the same conditions, and the same frail man. When I looked at him, however, there was a little glint in his eyes. He looked at me and scowled, "Son, I didn't do what you told me. You told me to listen to one of these tapes per day for six days until we got together again." He continued, "I didn't listen to one tape per day. I listened to all six tapes the first day, the second day, the third day, the fourth day, the fifth day, the sixth day, and today." He said, "Now, let me tell you what is going to happen. Next week when you come, I'll be sitting up in my bed. The next week, I'll be sitting next to my bed. The third week, I'll be sitting in my living room. After that, I'll be standing in your church telling your people about my healing."

That man prophesied his fate. The next week, he was sitting up in his bed. The week after that, he sat next to the bed. The third week, he was sitting in the living room. When I got there the fourth week, there was nobody home. The following week the judge showed up in my church, took a microphone, and proclaimed that the doctors in Houston had astonishingly proclaimed him cancer free.

Now, what happened to this judge? His cognitive dissonance (doubled-mindedness) had an emotional implantation. He came to a realization that things don't always have to be a certain way. Through the repetition and meditation (implantation) of the Word of God, it brought forth a new image on the inside of him and a confession of his mouth. This process brought forth a conation experience, transformed him by the renewing of his mind, and broke his limitation and brought, or attracted, his manifestation of healing.

This is God's will for your life: to not be conformed to this world's system, but to be transformed by the renewing of your mind that God can bring forth His manifestation in you. Your double-mindedness will give way to a revelation. That revelation, through repetition, will change the words of your mouth and break the limitations off of your life.

Now, I want to turn to the practical application of this process: biblical meditation, an intentional way to increase your faith.

KEYS

What does it mean to be a new creation in Christ? Meditate on 2 Corinthians 5:17.

Remember the "flesh" profits nothing, is contrary to God, and keeps you from doing God's will.

Remember the 4 C's to application in Romans 12:2:

1. Cognitive Dissonance— Don't be double-minded.

   Focus on God's truth.

   Meditate on it day and night (see the next chapter).

2. Confess God's Word—Confess it with imagination (see yourself according to the truth) and emotion (experience the emotion as if your truth has come to pass).

3. Consistency—Stay with your new truth until you've established a new personal belief system.

4. Conation—Do something deliberate and passionate every day to your most dominant thoughts.

Chapter 4

BARRIER BUSTERS
The Secret to the Law of Attraction

A FEW YEARS AGO, when I served as Campus Pastor of Oral Roberts University, I was doing some research for a book I was writing. I had traveled to Broken Arrow to one of my favorite bookstores to purchase some research materials. On my way back to Tulsa, it began to snow heavily. Now let me give you some advice. When it snows in Tulsa, GET OFF THE STREETS!!! The people in the South don't know how to drive in it.

As I was driving back, I looked up and saw a Sherman Tank, something like a 1970s Chevy, coming toward me. I later learned that the driver behind the wheel was a young teenager who had only had his license for a relatively short time. You can tell this was a bad scenario from the start. Without any warning, the young man hit an icy spot, spun out of control, slid across the dividing line, and hit me head on. The impact of the collision ricocheted me off of two other vehicles and knocked me fifty feet off the street into a snow-covered field. I was knocked unconscious. When I awoke, I didn't remember anything that had happened. All I knew was there was blood and glass everywhere, and I felt extreme pain on the left side of my body.

As a testimony to God's sustaining love, a Spirit-filled nurse had stopped at the scene of the accident. She waded through the snow and reached through the broken wreckage of the vehicle, praying over me while monitoring my vital signs. In a matter of moments EMSA arrived on the scene. My car was completely demolished. They had to remove the side of the vehicle with a chainsaw to extract me. They then raced me to the City of Faith Hospital.

As they wheeled me on a cart through the emergency room entrance, my wife, Judy, was already there waiting. The emergency team had contacted her and apprised her of the situation. When she looked down at me in the hospital, she was greeted by a face that was ripped to shreds, and by the blood and glass that were everywhere. Later a plastic surgeon on call would have to suture the pieces of my face back together. In perfect supernatural control, Judy took my hand and said, "Honey, God's here…everything's going to be all right."

Shortly after arriving, they ran a set of x-rays on me in the emergency room. After a while, the doctor came back holding an x-ray in her hand and said, "Mr. McIntosh, I'm sorry to tell you that you have a broken neck. You can see right here on the x-ray where the break is."

Very calmly, I asked her, "What does that mean for me?"

Standing out of my peripheral vision, the doctor mouthed the words to my wife, "It's not good."

They then took me upstairs to radiology to run a full set of x-rays on me. During that time, my friends from around the city started arriving at the hospital. Oral Roberts showed up. Along with him came his son Richard Roberts, President of Oral Roberts University, and his wife Lindsay, Pastor Billy Joe Daugherty, pastor of the 15,000 member Victory Christian Church, my brother Gary McIntosh, who pastors the largest church in the north side of Tulsa, and some others. Before they took the second set of x-rays, they all gathered around me to pray. (If you're going to have somebody pray for you for healing, it might as well be Oral Roberts.) I remember Oral Roberts taking my hand and declaring, "It's time to pray!" When he finished praying I didn't feel anything. I don't think he felt anything either, but I saw a flash vision of the basketball floor at ORU. I know it sounds like a strange way to get a touch from God, but inscripted down the side of the court was my fate: "Expect a Miracle." Somehow, I had a feeling everything was going to be all right.

A little while later the doctor came back in to see us. Now it was just Judy and me. Holding both sets of x-rays in her hand, she seemed confused. She looked at me and said, "Mr. McIntosh, this is somewhat confusing. Here are your two x-rays. You can see in the first x-ray where the break is. In the second x-ray we can't find any break whatsoever." That was a miraculous encounter that changed the course of my life forever. I had been healed!

There is a divine principle attached to this story. It is this: *if you can't see it, you can't receive it!* Faith is the product of a renewed mind that changes the way you see things. You need to see yourself according to God's truth, not simply according to fact. What you see in the natural is not how things really are. God sees from a spiritual perspective based on His truth and promises. He wants us to learn to change our perspective and focus on His Word. The fact is you might have cancer, but the truth is, you are healed by the stripes of Jesus. *Truth is stronger than fact.*

The truth is that God wants you to live a life without limits (John 10:10). The fact is most of us lead limited lives, even though we have a limitless Gospel. We seem to find ourselves stuck at the same point in our lives year after year. We are at the same point in our finances as we were last year at this time. Many people seem to end up at the same level in their health, their relationships, their ministries, their jobs, etc.

Now, if this is true, and God's real provision awaits us through this process of renewed thinking, the devil will do everything in his power to orchestrate the demolition of this process.

That is exactly what Paul addresses in 2 Corinthians 10:3-5:

> *For though we live in the world, we do not wage war as the world does. The weapons we fight with are not the weapons of the world. On the contrary, they have divine power to demolish strongholds. We demolish arguments and every pretension that sets itself up against the knowledge of God, and we take captive every thought to make it obedient to Christ.*

This is a passage about spiritual warfare, but it's not about going to the highest point in the city and yelling at the devil. It is about the battle that is waged in your thinking. If the devil can deceive us in our thinking, then he keeps us from receiving God's abundant provision.

Now notice Paul tells us the weapons of our warfare are not of this world's system. Why? Because all you can ever produce in your life springs from what system you believe in. This world's system is separated from God and can only produce what that system offers. Instead, the apostle Paul tells us we have divine power to demolish strongholds. A stronghold has taken root when we feel powerless to change, even though it is contrary to the Word of God. Paul adds to this stratagem; we demolish "arguments" ("imaginations" in the KJV). What is an argument? It is cognitive dissonance. It is two contrary opinions. It is double-mindedness (James 1:8). It is the contrary opinion that immobilizes us and results in un-productivity. "That man should not think he will receive anything from the Lord" (James 1:7).

The main weapon the enemy uses is double-mindedness. He causes this double-mindedness by using information or circumstances contradictory to God's truth. So on one hand, God reveals His truth to us. On the other hand, the enemy uses our environment to eradicate it. That is why people go away on a retreat and get their lives radically changed. However, when they return to their social environment, they go right back to their old lifestyle. Truth and fact collide and create a double-minded argument that seeks to immobilize our progress. Whichever side of the argument wins is the one that creates a picture in our heart. Because the enemy mainly uses the visible world, and God uses the invisible world, the argument is usually won by what is the easiest to focus on. That is why it is crucial for us to learn to see our world through God's perspective. A good example of this is found in 2 Kings 6:17. Elisha was surrounded by an army, and his servant was panicking, so Elisha prayed:

"And Elisha prayed, 'O LORD, open his eyes so he may see.' Then the LORD opened the servant's eyes, and he looked and saw the hills full of horses and chariots of fire all around Elisha." The servant saw the facts (the enemy had surrounded them), but Elisha *knew* the truth (the host of heaven was there to fight on their behalf).

Verse 5 reveals the last devastating strategy of the enemy: pretense. "Pretense" is knowledge that is based on assumption. "Assumption" is something that appears true, but may not be true. Sometimes it can even be a fact. The fact could be the doctor's report says "cancer," but the truth is you are healed by the stripes of Jesus (Isaiah 53:5; Matthew 8:17; 1 Peter 2:24).

The fact is, all of these "warfares" set themselves up against the "knowledge of God." In other words, you are up against an intentional strategy to dilute the effectiveness of the Word of God, to leave you impotent and unproductive. The process looks like this: the enemy brings a pretense or some assumption that you adopt as truth. That assumption results in an argument or a conflict in your thinking that produces an imagination or image inside of you. That image casts a stronghold that makes you think you can't really change your circumstances, or at least there's really no reason to believe things will ever be different.

We are now living in a time when this is more pronounced than ever. *The Harvard Medical Journal* states that 75 to 90 percent of all doctor related visits are stress related.[1] There is an undeniable link between our thinking and the results that occur in our bodies. Stress is not about our circumstances, but our perception of those circumstances. The same event may happen to two people, but have entirely different effects on each one. It is how they perceive them. The remedy for all this is in verse 5b, "…we take captive every thought to make it obedient to Christ." In other words, we have to recognize or re-cognate (rethink) our circumstances in line with biblical truth.

Now, that may seem like a daunting task ("to take captive every thought"). The fact is that we have 60,000 thoughts per day.[2] It seems improbable to be able to recognize every one of them. Here's how it works at least in part. When a circumstance happens, you experience a range of emotions. We've often been taught that emotions are bad, but in reality they reveal what we believe in that given moment. Let me give you an example. When I receive a bank statement that reveals less money than my ability to pay my obligations, even though it is not what I thought the facts were, it may cause me to panic if I'm not grounded in God's Word concerning provision. If I immediately look to God as my source, I have a kingdom mentality. If I get filled with anxiety about it, then I've got to make my thoughts obedient to the truth to receive God's provision, or act in a way to meet my obligations.

THE SOLUTION:
MIRROR, MIRROR ON THE WALL...

The question becomes, how do we do this? James 1:22-24 holds the answer: "But be doers of the Word, and not hearers only, deceiving your own selves. For if any be a hearer only and not a doer, he is like a man who looks at his face in the mirror, and after looking at himself, goes away and immediately forgets what he looks like" (author's combination of KJV and NIV).

A man who is a hearer of the Word, but doesn't apply it, is like a man who forgets the image in the mirror just cast of him. One of the first things you do when you get up in the morning is to look in the mirror. Do you like what you see? I don't know why, but there seems to be a metamorphous that transpires in the night time. A woman can go to bed looking like Pamela Anderson, but in the morning, suddenly she becomes the bride of Dracula. A man, similarly, goes to bed looking like Brad Pitt, but in the morning he more resembles Shrek. When I get up in the morning, it looks like someone electrocuted my hair. If I were to go in public like that, it would probably frighten little children and distress little old ladies.

So, when you look into a mirror, what do you do? You start to make adjustments, according to the new image you want. The Word of God is supposed to reflect back to you an image of who you really are. If you don't like who you are in some area, make adjustments according to the mirror of the Word.

An image is what you see. Each of us has our own self-image (how we view ourselves). Self-image is a predetermined belief of who we are right now and what we can become. It determines how we respond to others and how others respond to us. Self-image is the reflection to life that is mainly stored in our subconscious mind. Our lives are largely influenced by this internal picture we hold of ourselves. This picture controls our perception of how we see the events of life. Then, it sends a message to our emotional systems, physiological systems, and neurological systems to keep us aligned with that image.[3] When the subconscious mind perceives we are not on target with our self-image, it causes a stimulus or suppression of energy, ideas, and actions.[4] Self-image is an individual's mental and spiritual concept or picture of himself, which is the real key to performance.[5] Self-image sets boundaries for our accomplishments. It defines what you can and cannot do.[6]

In other words, your subconscious mind's job is to keep in line with your image of yourself in your heart. That's why people sabotage themselves and end up some place they don't want to be. You can never rise above the image you have of yourself. Changing how you see yourself is where all transformation begins. Renewed thinking only works when it is consistent with our self-image. *Principles don't change a person; images do.*

Changing your image engages something called the reticular activating system (RAS), or your recognition system (see page 46). Through positive focusing, negative filtering, and individual perception, your RAS brings forth a recognition and attraction of people, ideas, and resources in your environment that are necessary for you to reach your objective. In short, your image affects every realm of your success and productivity. The question becomes: what is the source of your image?

Let's again look at Genesis 1:26. "Then God said, 'Let Us make man in Our *image,* according to Our likeness; let them have dominion…'" (NKJV). God made man in His image and likeness. Remember, the term *image* means "reflection or resemblance."[7] *Likeness* gives you the idea of "to model, shape, fashion, manner, similitude, or pattern."[8] *Image* is the nature of God, and *likeness* is the function of God.

Now let me break this down in a way that can bring some practicality to all of this. The word *nature* means "inborn character, innate disposition, inherent tendencies, instincts, essential qualities or attributes." The idea of *function* is "the normal or characteristic action, performance, course of work."[9] In other words, by the very fact of creation, you have been engineered for success.

God placed His very nature in you. You have the inborn character, disposition, inherent tendencies, instincts, desires, and attributes of God. If that weren't enough, He gave you the ability to function or to manifest these qualities.

If this is true, then what happened to humankind? Genesis 3:1-10 talks about the "Fall" of man. Eve submitted to the serpent's wiles and partook of the Tree of the Knowledge of Good and Evil. After Adam and Eve "fell," they suddenly noticed they were naked, so they hid and fashioned clothes for themselves. They saw themselves (their image) differently.

The "Fall" of man distorted his view of himself. Who you are depends on what you see. When man puts a limit on what he *can* be, he puts a limit on what he *will* be. Jesus came to restore His image in us (see 2 Corinthians 3:1-18; James 1:21-24; Romans 8:29; 1 Corinthians 15:49; 2 Corinthians 4:4; Colossians 1:27; Colossians 3:10; Hebrews 1:3).

Maxwell Maltz, in his breakthrough book *Psycho-Cybernetics,* says it this way: "Self-image is the individual's mental and spiritual concept or picture of himself, which is the real key to behavior."[10] Self-image sets boundaries for individual performance and accomplishments. It defines what you can or cannot do. If you expand your self-image, you can expand any area of your life. A positive image can imbue a person with new capabilities and talents, and literally turn failure into success.[11] Renewed thinking works when it is consistent with the individual's self-image.[12] Your self-image is not transformed by knowledge, but by thinking and experiencing it.[13] All your actions, feelings, and behaviors are always consistent with your self-image. It is really impossible to act otherwise.[14] A human being always acts in accordance to what he believes is true about himself.[15] Amazingly, your nervous system cannot tell the difference between what is real or imagined.[16] Before a person can change, they must see themselves in a new image.

Now, let's put all these thoughts in perspective. God made you in His image and likeness; He made you in His nature and function. It helps me to know I'm made in the reflection and resemblance of God. But what does that really mean to me? The term *image* is also the root for *imag-ination.* Imagination is the ability to think without limitation. As long as your imagination is based on truth, it is helpful; otherwise, it is just mere fantasy. The ability to be productive and to dominate your environment is based on your ability to break the limits off your thinking and regain your God-image. The Creator of the universe engineered you for success and achievement.

Let me give you an example. Imagine if you were to come into a certain church service where they usually have prayer for the sick. Let's say they ask for people who need a touch from God, and 100 people raise their hands. After they pray, they ask all those who received a healing of some sort to come forward and testify of the results, and ten people come forward. The next week is the same scenario, with the same results: 100/10. The following week, the same: 100/10. Pretty soon the image you hold in your mind about healing is about 10 percent of the people get touched. Suddenly, your touch from God becomes like the lottery. You raise your hand, hoping you'll be in the lucky 10 percent, but chances are, it's not going to be you. The fact is, 10 percent did get healed, but the truth is you already are healed by the stripes of Jesus. Truth is stronger than fact, but it takes an image of transformation to appropriate it.

The difference between people who are successful and productive, and those who are not, is that successful people "see" themselves bigger than their problems; unsuccessful people do not. It is a matter of perspective. For instance, use a scale of 1 to 10 (10 being the highest) and imagine you're a level 3 person. If you face a level 6 problem, it may seem devastating. If, however, you are a level 8 person, the same level 6 problem would not seem perplexing. It is truly a matter of perspective and capacity.[17] Now the problem is no problem at all.

This is what I call the "Austin Powers" philosophy. It is the curse of "mini-me." You fail to see the true image of who you are in Christ. The problem looms bigger than it really is, and it defeats you. Successful people always focus on solutions, not problems. They don't focus on the natural realm to supply their needs. Instead, they look to that invisible realm where God's provisions have an eternal source of supply.

Many people fail to appropriate what's rightfully theirs simply because their self-image is dwarfed. It creates set-points or self-limiting beliefs that put a ceiling on our lives. Self-image (how I *see* myself) creates self-esteem (how I *feel about* myself). When these two factors operate negatively in our lives, they create a lack of impetus to step up and try what we may know is the will of God for our lives and are the keys to our success (in chapter 5 we'll consider the five sources of all self-limiting beliefs).

Where do poor self-image and low self-esteem come from? Generally, they are conditioned from our childhood. A child is born with no self-image. Every idea, opinion, feeling, attitude, or value is learned from childhood experience. Everything you are today is the result of an idea or impression you accepted as true.[18] When you believe something to be true, it becomes true for you. "You are not what you *think* you are; what you *think,* you *are*.[19]

If in your formative years you received 20 no's for every yes, or 10 "you're being wrong" for every 1 "you're doing it right," and 5 "you're stupid" for 1 "you're awesome," you're likely conditioned with low self-image and esteem.[20] These negative messages generally create comfort zones, set-points, or self-sabotaging actions that hold you back in life. For many people, the feeling of unworthiness makes them feel it is inappropriate for them to be blessed or rewarded for their efforts. They often position themselves to line up with their unworthy self-image (self-worth or the lack of it) and create the comfort zone of mediocrity or failure. It unfortunately becomes a self-perpetuating cycle that often leads to despair or self-perpetuating stagnations.

One of the stages for transforming your personal belief system is to imagine Jesus stepping into your life. A woman I was helping once could not imagine that being true. Her religious background had thoroughly conditioned her to think she was too unworthy to have Him in her life. Once she overcame this barrier, her new image catapulted her forward in every arena in her life.

Your beliefs about yourself and your world create levels of expectation. Expectations determine attitudes, and attitudes determine behavior (what you will or will not do). If you go back to the beginning of creation in Genesis 1, you will find how God created. When He created anything, He spoke to the source, and out of the source came the thing. For instance, when He created plants, He spoke to the ground, and out of the ground came the plant. When He created the fish, He spoke to the water, and out of the water came the fish. My good friend Myles Munroe states it this way: "What happens when you remove the thing from its source? It dies!" If you remove the fish from the water, it dies. If you remove the plant from the soil, it dies. Therefore, Genesis's definition of death is separation from its source.

When God made man and woman, what source did He speak to? Genesis 1:26 tells us He spoke to Himself. What happens when a man or woman is separated from God? He or she dies! You might think, "I know a lot of people separated from God who aren't dead." Perhaps they're not dead physically, but they are dead inside. They've lost the image of God. They are spiritually dead.

Let me show you the effects of this understanding. If we walk according to our flesh, we *will* experience serious repercussions. Romans 8:5-6 states, "Those who live according to the (flesh) have their minds set on what that nature desires; but those who live in accordance with the Spirit have their minds set on what the Spirit desires. The mind of sinful man (flesh—doing God's will, your way; for example, love versus lust) is death…."

In other words, the mind of the flesh is death—separation from its source. Believers who operate in the flesh are separated from their true source, and therefore cannot receive from God whatever they need from their source. So, no matter how much you want God's provision, and no matter how much God wants to give it to you, you can't receive it because you are separated from the source of its manifestation.

OVERCOMING LIFE'S GIANTS

We can see this in a clear example from Hebrew culture. Numbers 13:1-2 says, "The LORD said to Moses, 'Send some men to explore the land of Canaan, which I am giving to the Israelites.'"

It is clear from this passage that God intended to give Canaan (the Promised Land) to Israel. Moses then sent out twelve spies to explore the land. They brought back glowing reports of a land filled with milk and honey. It was bountiful and contained everything they would ever need. They brought back a cluster of grapes so large it took two men to carry them on a pole. We're talking about some significant grapes! It was a land that was beyond their wildest imagination.

Yet, when it came time to give their report on the land, here's what was said: "But the people who live there are powerful, and the cities are fortified and very large. We saw the descendents of Anak there" (Numbers 13:28). In this country lived the Amalekites, the Hittites, the Jebusites, the Amorites, the Canaanites, the "uptites," "out of sites," and "mosquito bites." All the "ites" lived there. There was great opposition in the land.

The ten spies gave what the writer of Numbers calls an "evil report." They spread a bad report that stirred fear amongst the people. They even included this phrase, "The land we explored devours those living in it." They were declaring that the people inhabiting Canaan were giants. Then this amazing revelation came forth: "We seemed like grasshoppers *in our own eyes,* and we looked the same to them" (Numbers 13:28-33).

Now, notice the image they had of themselves. "They looked like giants, and we seemed like grasshoppers *in our own eyes.*" They had spent the last 400 years in Egyptian captivity, and even though they were liberated from Egypt (slavery), they couldn't get Egypt out of their hearts. They still saw themselves as lowly slaves in their own eyes. Their image of themselves created a cognitive dissonance (double-mindedness) in them. Even though God had blessings of unparalleled proportions waiting for them in the Promised Land, their negative image prevented them from walking into the fullness of it. Suddenly, in chapter 14, they began to declare, "If we'd only died in Egypt!" "Wouldn't it be better for us to go back to Egypt?"

A low self-image will always cause people to develop a "GB," a *"Going Back,"* to an old comfort zone or set-point. People will literally sabotage themselves to stay there.

The devil's strategy is to blind the minds of people (2 Corinthians 4:3, 4; 1 Corinthians 2:9-16). It doesn't say he wants to blind the eyes of people; he *works* to blind their minds. Remember, you don't see things as *they* are, you see things as *you* are.

Years ago, when I worked at Oral Roberts University, we set up ministry teams that traveled all over the nation. My family and I met up with one of the teams in the Bronx, New York. Our target was to go into locales and draw people with up-beat music and then minister truth to them. We really had some "hot" musicians who were playing some "hot" music. The music wasn't like "Sweet Hour of Prayer"—it was more like "Devil, I'm going to rip your lips off."

The group set up in a park in the Bronx that was nothing more than a cement slab with a few swing sets. The group started playing and soon a crowd gathered. After about twenty minutes, I took the microphone and shared how Jesus could radically change their lives, and a proportionately large number of people made decisions for transformation.

The next day we set up in the tenements. As the students were setting up the stage, I looked around and saw every excessive indulgence you can imagine. To my right they were pimping. They were selling drugs to my left, and doing drugs not far from me…all in the eye-shot of police, and nobody seemed to care.

At the appropriate time, the team began to play a worship set. Again, people started hanging out of windows to listen and gathered around the platform. Only this time, it wasn't such a friendly crowd. The crowd began to pelt the group with glass. Fearing for their safety, I cried out, "Lord, what do You want me to do?"

In my spirit I felt the Lord say, "If you get up and prophesy, I'll change the atmosphere of this place." Without hesitation, I bounded onto the stage, grabbed a microphone, and blurted out, "Thus says the Lord, someone here is on drugs…." Now, how's that for a revelation? I thought to myself, *and…Lord, everybody here's probably on drugs.* Then the rest of it came: "You're on your way to commit suicide at this very moment. But I, the Lord, intercept you in your destruction right now."

The moment I said it, a young man fell to the ground and started weeping in agony. It turned out that he was a heroin and cocaine addict. His drug habit was so expensive, he had no means to pay for his fixes. In desperation, he was on his way to the subway to throw himself in front of a subway train. People quickly gathered around to minister to him. He was marvelously set free, saved, and filled with the Holy Spirit.

We later learned that not only was he an addict, but so was his father and his father's father. That low image had plagued three generations. His image of himself had been the same all his life: it's never going to be different than it is right now. In the middle of his desperation, God met and set his life on a new course. At the same time, the event of that day calmed the crowd and opened the door to multiple transformations among the people in the tenements. The Lord opened this young man's mind, created a new image in his life, and sent him on his way redeemed, with a new perspective about himself.

Media and television know the value of image. That's what "television" is. It is telling you a vision. That's why young girls see Brittany Spears and change their dress style. It is what car advertisers do. They let you picture yourself in their vehicle, projecting what you most want, repetitively, until you feel you've got to have it.

Now, here is an amazing fact: once your subconscious mind is locked onto a "truth" (real or imagined), it tends to block out all information contrary to that belief. It is what psychologists call "Scotoma," or blind spots. There literally are beliefs that are holding you back, and you are oblivious to them. Even though God created you to be in control of your life, life seems to dictate to you. How can you turn this process around and transform your personal belief system? How can you break the frustrating ceiling of failure, mediocrity, or stagnation?

The amazing process of lifting the limits off of your life is mapped out in such a way you can do it automatically.

Let me lay out a set of core principles to change what you believe, what you see, what you expect, and what you will do *(remember, principles don't change a person, images do)*.

IMAGINE THE POSSIBILITIES

There is a way to intentionally increase your faith and change your image of yourself. Proverbs 4:20-23 says: "My son, pay attention (or attend) to what I say (to my words); listen closely to my words. Do not let them out of your sight, keep them within your heart; for they are life to those who find them and health to a man's whole body. Above all else, guard your heart, for (your heart) is the wellspring (or boundaries) of (your) life." (Added emphasis is mine added from other translations.)

Here are the principles:

Pay attention to God's words and concepts. Literally, this means "to attend, meditate, wait upon or imagine God's Word."[21] If you don't see it, you can't receive it. For instance, if you see giving or tithing as depletion, you will never do it. You must see life through faith that has focused itself on the truth. Study all the scriptures that bring increase. (See my web-site for the *Barrier Busters Manual* to give you all the scriptures to overcome the barriers in your life, or see the following Appendix at the end of this chapter.)

Do not let them out of your sight. Repetition is the key to the reinforcement of truth. It takes 21 days to create a new habit or to create a new belief system. (I'll give you the application at the end of this chapter.)

Keep it in your heart. Renew the soul chamber of your heart to the truth that is in your spirit. Let your conscious mind assimilate ultimate truth, and through repetition get it into your subconscious mind and set up an automatic response system that will change your present self-limiting beliefs. (Again, I'll show you the direct application at the end of this chapter.)

This is primarily done through your confession. Confession by itself will get it into your belief system 10 percent. Confession with imagination brings it into your personal belief system 55 percent. Confession, imagination, and emotion will get truth into your personal belief system 100 percent.[22]

This process is life, health, and boundary-breaking in your life. It makes life vibrant, fresh, and strong.

Jesus gives us great insight into how truth can set us free: "Then said Jesus to those Jews which believed on him, 'If ye continue in my word, then are ye my disciples indeed; And ye shall know the truth, and the truth shall make you free'" (John 8:31, 32).

Please notice: truth does not set you free. It is the truth you "know" that sets you free. This term *know* means "to know, recognize, understand, perceive."[23] This word gives you the idea to lie down with or to give birth to: the root of the word means "to know experientially."[24] The implication of this word gives you the idea of getting "pregnant" by it. The point is obvious; the Word that sets you free is one that through intimacy becomes your own. In essence, you get pregnant with the truth of God's Word. It can't be Joyce Meyer's word, or James Robison's perspective, or Myles Munroe's revelation. It can't be Benny Hinn's insight; it has to be the Word inside of you.

Now, exactly how does this happen to us? How do we become so intimate with truth that it transforms us into a different person?

> "Blessed is the man who does not walk in the counsel of the wicked or stand in the way of sinners or sit in the seat of mockers. But, his delight is in the Law of the LORD, and on His Law he meditates day and night. He is like a tree planted by streams of water, which yields its fruit in season and whose leaf does not wither. Whatever he does prospers." (Psalm 1:1-3)

The Psalmist begins by declaring, *"Blessed* is the man…." The term *blessed* means "empowered to prosper, to favor, render successful, increase, advancing in growth or wealth, gain in anything good or desirable, successful progress, attainment of the object desired."[25] One person said it this way, "Prosperity is the ability to use God's ability to meet any need."

Blessed (having the ability to use God's ability to meet my need) is the person who:

Does not walk in the counsel of the wicked—who does not cultivate the world's system, because all you can ever produce is what that system can produce. That system collides with the kingdom of God.

Does not walk in the way of sinners—what is the way of sinners? It is the flesh and unbelief. Such action profits nothing, is contrary to God, and the things you want to do you cannot do (John 6:63; Romans 7; Galatians 5:16, 17).

Does not sit in the seat of mockers—mocking what? Mocking the truth of God's Word. All such activity short-circuits the provisions of the kingdom. Mockery listened to repeatedly (through all its forms, media, from authority figures or peers, etc.) brings contempt, or at best confusion, to the truth.

Instead, his "delight is in the law of the Lord." The term *delight* means "to have a high degree of satisfaction, to desire that which is precious or valuable, pursuit."[26] I once had a college professor who told me it means you can't get enough of it. It's like a football "junkie" on New Year's Day. He has four large screen TV sets going at the same time. He can't quite get enough of football. Or, it's like a woman at a sale in the mall. She will "shop until she drops."

The Psalmist tells us to eliminate the negatives and accentuate the positives, and delight and pursue God's laws. What is a law? A law is a principle that tells you how a thing works best. How do you pursue these laws? By meditating on this law day and night.

The term *meditate* means "to mutter, to utter, murmur, ponder, stretch, see beyond, muse, or imagine."[27] This meditation means to mutter or utter. If we take an honest look at what we say on any given day, we already are muttering and uttering, "I can't believe what she did to me. Can you believe it? I was minding my own business when all of a sudden…." Do you get the picture? If we're going to mutter, we might as well do it according to the truth.

It also means to ponder, or muse. As you dwell on God's truth, it causes you to see and stretch beyond where you are. This word also means to imagine. To imagine means to think without limitation. It means to see yourself according to truth (in the positive sense). Albert Einstein once said, "Imagination is more important than knowledge. Imagination is everything."[28] It is a preview of coming attractions. As you see yourself according to truth, it creates a new image on the inside of you. Your subconscious mind then works to make that image come to pass. It remedies your present situations. Biblical meditation is a way to intentionally increase your faith.

Before you start to worry that this is New Age or Transcendental Meditation, let me assure you that it is not. Remember, satan is not a creator. All he can do is imitate and pervert truth. Don't let his deception rob you of the "missing ingredient" to transform your personal belief system. It is the Bible that encourages meditation—continual "musing" on God's Word, which is inspired by the Holy Spirit (2 Timothy 3:16).

The Psalmist says a person should meditate "day and night." What does this mean? Quite simply, start your day and end your day in biblical meditation. Why? Because when you start your day looking into the perfect law of freedom (see James 1:22-24), you begin to see yourself according to the real truth, which the enemy will contest all day long. When you end your day, meditating in the Word will regroup the same truth the enemy has sought to steal from you all day long. Another reason to end your day in biblical meditation is that your subconscious mind never turns off. As you feed it truth, it dwells on it all night long.

That's why sometimes you go to bed thinking about a situation, and the next morning you wake up with the solution.

Now, look at these amazing results this process provides:

He is like a tree planted by streams of water. Like the vine and branches described in John 15, you are connected to the Ultimate Source of Life. You are connected to the right system. When the Psalmist talks of water, the idea is water that flows in canals or used for irrigation. This source of sustenance (God's Word) is what causes you to flourish.

You yield fruit. When you are connected to the true Source of Life, you will bring forth the desired manifestations in every area of your life.

Whose leaf does not wither. It does not wither in times of drought, or dryness.

Whatever he does prospers. This person is favored, rendered successful, advanced in growth or wealth, gains the thing desired, makes successful progress, uses their ability to use God's ability to meet any need.

What an incredible picture! If we avoid living in the world's system and instead meditate on the truth of the laws that tell us how a thing works best, we will bring forth fruitful manifestation, attract the kingdom of heaven, flourish, and live a life of advancement and increase. This is the Law of Attraction at work. James Allen said, "A man is literally what he thinks. His character is the sum total of his thoughts." This is why biblical meditation is the missing ingredient. When we allow the Word to dominate our thoughts and get into our hearts, it will create action that will break the shackles of mediocrity, or stagnation.

That is the sum total of the story of the boy with epileptic seizures found in Mark 9. Whenever a seizure would occur, it would throw the boy to the ground and cause him to foam at the mouth. The boy's disgruntled father came to Jesus and said that His disciples could not cast out the demon. Jesus ultimately responded by saying, "All things are possible for those that believe." The father of the boy responded, "I do believe, help me overcome my unbelief." In essence he was saying, "I know what I hear. How do I get it to work?"

That is the heart of this book, which brings us to the last set of principles (before we look at very practical applications):

> "Do not let this Book of the Law depart out of your mouth; meditate on it day and night, so that you may be careful to do everything written in it. Then you will be prosperous and you will have (good, KJV) success." Joshua 1:8

Here Joshua amplifies five key principles:

Confession—Your confession must add to itself imagination and emotion to get into your personal belief system 100 percent.

Incubation—This, again, is the principle of biblical meditation. There are approximately twenty-seven different terms used in the Bible for meditation, and over several hundred references. Meditation is a way to intentionally increase your faith, or to attract God's kingdom.

Revelation—Incubation gives way to revelation. Revelation is something you always knew but never realized. You may know God as a healer. Suddenly, you realize He is *your* healer. You may know God as a Savior. Suddenly, you realize He is *your* Savior. Suddenly, what you "know," you realize belongs to *you*.

Impartation—Your revelation gives way to impartation. What you realize must become part of you.

Manifestation—What is on the inside of you manifests on the outside of you. You attract the kingdom of heaven.

THE MISSING INGREDIENT

The missing ingredient to transforming your personal belief system is biblical meditation. According to our definition of biblical meditation, there are five stages in its process. Amazingly, the first four correspond to the four major chambers of your brain. Let's consider now the progression of the five stages:

Five Stages of Biblical Meditation

1. **Still Stage** (Psalm 46:10)

   "Be still and know that I am God."

   Still in this passage means to "cease, draw toward, relax or desist."[29]

   The root to this term is *rapha.* This is the Hebrew term for "to heal, cure, repair, pardon or comfort." The still stage is what psychologists call "alpha state." Alpha state is that state between being asleep and awake.

   This is the state when your subconscious mind is most influenced. This is the stage of relaxation, praise and worship, healing and receptivity.

1. **Medulla**—The job of the Medulla is to regulate bodily functions.

2. **Imagination Stage** (Psalm 1:2, 3)

   This is the place where you create emotions with dominant images in your thinking. Here's where you re-set set-points.
   In this stage the conscious mind chooses the new truth of Scripture, and through repetition this truth goes into your personal belief system in the subconscious mind. Here is where confession, imagination, and emotion change your beliefs.

2. The **Amygdala's** job is to compare new data.

3. **Strategy Stage** (Joshua 1:8)

   Based on the truth that I see, what should I do? Here's where you write out a plan for action. Your action plan should have five parts:

   1. A vision (what I want to do and what I want to be)
   2. A theme (a succinct expression of the vision for remembrance)

3. The **Cerebral Cortex's** job is to create strategy.

3. Objectives (goals to make your dreams come true)
4. Strategies (steps to your objectives)
5. Priorities (what do I focus on right now— the act of writing goals is proven to increase the likelihood of success by 1,000 percent.)[30]

4. **Action (Application) Stage**

The action stage is the place where I do something *every day* toward my highest priority.

The difference between the strategy and the action stage is the "fleshing" out of what's on paper.

5. **Thanksgiving Stage**

Thanksgiving is the act of thanking God for your goals becoming a reality. Why? Because according to Philippians 4:6, 7: "Do not be anxious about anything, but in everything, by prayer and petition, with thanksgiving, present your requests

4. The **Frontal Lobe** is the decision maker.

to God. And the peace of God, which transcends all understanding, will guard your hearts and your minds in Christ Jesus."

Thanksgiving puts a guard over your heart and mind. In other words, the act of thanksgiving protects what you place in your mind and your heart. Your feelings are a feedback mechanism to what you truly believe. Your thoughts create feelings, and your feelings solidify what your thoughts say is true. Feelings give courage to your heart to try to reach your goal.

Once you discover your set-point or self-limiting beliefs, then find the antidote in God's Word. For instance, if your limitation is lack, then your antidote is prosperity. If your barrier is sickness, your antidote of truth is healing. For doubt, it's faith; for fear it's love. For guilt, fear, and inferiority, it's righteousness. (You can find a list of self-limiting beliefs and antidotes in the *Barrier Busters Manual*. See Appendix at the end of this Chapter.)

Once you see yourself according to the truth, then what strategy do you need to work on? Your strategy may include preparation for a new job, reading about an effective diet plan, changing your exercise regimen, or learning about investments and stewardship.

The final key is to do something every day toward your highest priority. The process of manifestation is: thoughts lead to emotions, emotions lead to solidifying your will, a solid will leads to actions, and actions bring results. As much as I believe in meditation and confession, as far as I can tell, neither of them on their own brings manifestation.[31] It takes action to succeed. The bridge between the inner world and the outer world is action.[32] It is the action that brings results.

Finally, thanksgiving puts a guard over your heart and mind. Thanksgiving helps "cement" your soul chamber to the spirit chamber of your heart, particularly the subconscious mind. The subconscious mind can't tell the difference between what is real and what is imagined. Once it accepts what is truth, it works to bring it to pass. This thanksgiving stage is an essential part of the process (Ron McIntosh Ministries has nine biblical meditation tapes called "Barrier Busters" that walk people through this five-fold process.) What you think about and thank about, comes about.[33]

I was sharing this process in a seminar setting, and I asked if anyone had any questions. A woman stood up and said, "Yeah, I've got a question about how this works. I want to lose weight. Does this work for that?"

As she was speaking, I could see people nodding their heads, like, "Yeah, does it work for that?" Unmoved, I just asked this simple question, "What is the antidote for weight loss?"

Almost indignantly the woman responded, "Eat less."

Everyone laughed, including me, but I replied, "As long as you think that, you'll never lose weight." I continued, "Let me walk you through this five-fold process."

You can create self-empowering beliefs through biblical meditation. Generally, the real biblical antidote is found in love, righteousness, and self-control. So, your steps are these:

1. Get still.

2. See yourself according to the truth of the Scripture concerning love, righteousness, and self-control. First, God loves you just as you are. Second, you are in right standing with God not by your action, but based on what Jesus did for you. Receive it by faith. Third, see yourself according to your ideal weight. (I'm not talking about some phony image of when you were sixteen years old, but a realistic idea or picture of where you are heading now.) This is where your confession comes into play. "I am excited about feeling fit at (your ideal weight) pounds."

3. Create a strategy of how to get there. For this woman, I drew the Mediterranean Diet out for her on the board:

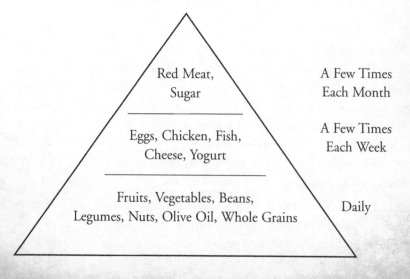

4. Action Stage converts it to something like this:

On Monday, I'll eat… (four small meals accordingly).

On Tuesday, I'll eat… on Wednesday I'll eat…, etc.

5. Give thanks to God that He is doing this (present tense) in your life.

Every person in that audience wanting to lose weight was scrambling for pen and paper to take notes. Later, I told my staff about what had transpired in the seminar. My former office manager was an attractive woman, but she was not pleased with her weight gain in recent years. Somewhat regularly she had said that she wanted to lose thirty or forty pounds. Shortly after this, her husband took a job in Phoenix, and she moved away. A little over a year later they moved back to my hometown of Tulsa. Shortly thereafter, she showed up at my office. When she walked through the door, I looked at her and said, "Where is the rest of you? You've lost a lot of weight."

She grinned and said, "Yeah, I lost forty pounds."

I said, "How did you do it?"

She then went through a brief description of walking out these five steps. She found her self-empowering beliefs, meditated on them, along with a visualization of her at her ideal weight. She then set out a strategy diet (remember the term *diet* means "lifestyle," not a short process of deprivation). She then redid her grocery shopping and set out a menu for every week. Feeling empowered to do what she wanted, she followed through on her plan. The result was an amazing transformation to her ideal weight. Today she is still thanking God.

I have seen countless people transform their lives in a number of different areas. I've seen unstable people transformed into confident, thriving individuals. I've seen people break through and overcome limitations in financial arenas, health, being at peace, feeling loved, feeling forgiven of past indiscretions, and overcoming fear, doubt, and stress. The list is endless, because God's Word is limitless.

To really understand set-points and self-limiting beliefs, we need to understand how they originate in our thinking. So, now we need to turn our attention to busting the barriers of self-limiting beliefs.

KEYS
BARRIER BUSTERS

Remember, you've got to see it to receive it. Biblical meditation allows you to see yourself according to the truth.

Remember the devil's four strategies to keep you stagnant in self-limiting beliefs:

> strongholds
>
> arguments
>
> imaginations
>
> pretense

Make sure you see yourself through the mirror of God's Word, not the mirror of experience.

Biblical meditation is the key to transforming your personal belief system.

Remember the five stages of biblical meditation:

> Get still with some peaceful music or relaxation exercises.
>
> Imagination—Once you've discovered your self-limiting beliefs (see Appendix at the end of this chapter), see yourself according to the antidote. If it is prosperity, how does that look to

you? Remember, your subconscious mind can't tell the difference between real or imagined. It simply goes to work to make it come to pass. Part of believing is "make-believing."

Strategy—You'll start attracting people, ideas, and resources to your most dominant thoughts (check my website for seminars toward this end). Do the following exercise:

What I most want or want to overcome: _____

_____

_____

_____

_____

VISION:

OBJECTIVES:

PRIORITIES & TIMELINE:

What am I doing daily toward this goal?

   * Day 1

   * Day 2

   * Day 3

   * Day 4

   * Day 5

   * Day 6

   * Day 7

Every day do something toward your highest priority.

Now thank Him! Thank Him for the truth that is alive in you and is happening right now. Affirm to yourself that God's truth is acting on your behalf. Thank Him that your breakthrough is happening. Remember, you are unstoppable!

APPENDIX

Self-Limiting Beliefs	Antidotes
1. Fear, anger, rage, unforgiveness, guilt, lust	1. Love—(sometimes combined with righteousness and forgiveness)
2. Discouragement (dis-courage), unhappiness, grief	2. Joy—(sometimes combined with righteousness)
3. Anxiety, worry, guilt, stress	3. Peace—(sometimes combined with righteousness)
4. Frustration, desire to quit	4. Patience—(sometimes combined with righteousness)

5. Doubt, unbelief, fear, unfaithfulness

6. Flesh (man's attempt to do God's will), out-of-control urges

7. Sickness, disease (dis-ease)

8. Resentment, anger, hatred

9. Guilt, inferiority, fear, condemnation

10. Lack, poverty, stagnation financially

11. Inability to break through

12. Selfishness, pride, double-mindedness

5. Faith—(sometimes combined with righteousness)

6. Self-control (combined with righteousness and grace)

7. Healing (sometimes combined with righteousness and forgiveness)

8. Forgiveness (sometimes combined with righteousness and love)

9. Righteousness

10. Prosperity—(sometimes combined with righteousness)

11. Grace—(sometimes combined with righteousness)

12. Goodness, kindness, gentleness combination

Chapter 5

BREAKING SELF-LIMITING BELIEFS

THE BOOK *THE SECRET* SAYS, "The Law of Attraction is 'like attracting like.'"[1]

Everything coming to you, you are attracting into your life.[2] Thoughts become things.[3]

The Secret also says, "The real problem is that most people are thinking about what they don't want, and they wonder why it shows up over and over."[4] The only reason people don't have what they want is because they are thinking more about what they don't want.[5] This is called the "don't want" epidemic.

The fact of the matter is the Law of Attraction works when dominant images create set-points, and people will act according to the way they see themselves in their heart. You can never rise above the image you have of yourself in your heart.

There is an amazing story about a woman who suffered from amnesia. The story is about a thirty-year-old woman who was married with two children. Like many people, she grew up in a home where she was criticized and unfairly treated by her parents. As a result, she developed deep-seated feelings of inferiority and low self-esteem. She was shy, negative, fearful, and had no confidence. She felt unworthy and totally invaluable. She thought she had no real talent (for anything).

One day while driving to the store, another car ran a red light and smashed into her vehicle. When she awoke in the hospital, she had suffered a concussion and had complete memory loss. She had all of her physical faculties, but every memory of her former life was gone. She was a total amnesiac.

Through a series of extensive tests, the doctors determined her memory loss was complete. Her husband and children visited her daily, but she had no recollection of them. The case was so unusual, doctors and specialists came from all over to visit her and examine her unusual condition.

Ultimately, she went home, but her memory was still a complete blank. Determined to understand what happened to her, she began to study everything she could about the subject of amnesia. She met and spoke with a number of specialists in this field. Eventually, she wrote a treatise about all her findings. Some time later, she was invited to a medical convention to address the subjects of amnesia and neurological functionality.

From the time of the accident and through her recovery, something astonishing took place. She became a completely different person. All of the positive attention from the hospital and the love and support from her family made her feel valuable. The attention, acclaim, and esteem from the medical community elevated her self-respect. She was transformed into a positive, confident, outgoing, in-demand speaker and authority in the medical community.

All the memory of her negative childhood had been wiped out. Along with it, her feelings of inferiority were eradicated. She became an entirely new person.[6] Usually when I tell this story, I ask the question, "How many of you know someone who needs amnesia?" It is humorous, but true. It is what the Scottish philosopher David Hume called the Blank Slate.[7] The idea is that every person is born into this world with no thought or idea, and everything a person becomes is learned from infancy onward. The adult becomes the sum total of what they learn, feel, and experience from childhood to present.[8]

The blueprint of your life is primarily the "programming" you received in your past from your childhood. Your home, school, parents, friends, and teachers are all influential in creating mind-sets and expectations in your life. If they are positive reflections of the truth, that is wonderful, but often they are incorrect distortions of truth that lead to self-limiting beliefs or set-points that can negatively impact a person's life for years. A person becomes conditioned to an automatic response that then runs their life.

The real question is, where do these limitations come from? Why do you think and act differently from the neighbor you grew up with? The storage bin of your thinking comes primarily from five sources:

1. Social environment

2. Authority figures

3. Self-image

4. Repetitious information

5. Experience

Let's look at how these *five areas* help formulate our thinking and our image of ourselves, which is our *personal belief system.*[9]

AREA #1
SOCIAL ENVIRONMENT

Environment includes the conditions, circumstances, and influences surrounding and affecting a person.[10] The animated movie *The Lion King* depicts this principle beautifully. Simba is born into the world as the son of the king. (Does this sound familiar?) His uncle Scar is upset that he has lost his place in succession to the throne to young Simba. He plots to kill the king, Mufasa, Simba's father. He not only succeeds, but through lies and deception he also convinces Simba to feel responsible for his father's death. Remorseful and humiliated, Simba flees to escape the overwhelming guilt of his seeming misdeed. For a while he hides from responsibility in obscurity with his new friends Timon and Pumba.

In time, he grows up carefree, trying to forget his past. Years later, his childhood sweetheart, Nala, looking for help in her troubled home-land, stumbles into Simba. With romance rekindling, the dialog goes something like this. Nala asks, "Simba, where have you been all these years? We've really needed you."

Simba's response is startling and typical. "No one needs me."

Nala responds, "You're the king!"

Simba protests, "No, I'm not." Then he shouts, "Hakuna Mattata!"

This is a Swahili phrase that depicts a carefree lifestyle and means "There are no worries here" (just excuses).

Then Simba continues, "Sometimes bad things happen, and you can't do anything about them."

Isn't that how most of us feel? Bad things have happened to us in our past, and there's nothing we can do about them. Unfortunately, for many people the past also seems to rob them of the resolve to do something about their present.

At this point Nala is confused and responds, "You're not the Simba I remember."

Often our past creates images of fears, guilt, and worries that begin to dictate what we will or will not try in the future.

Simba, dejected and facing the confusing emotions of his past, responds, "You're right, I'm not."

How often have learned fears crippled us from the willingness to step out into our destiny? How many times have we allowed past shortcomings to cause us to forget who we are in Jesus?

Reflecting in anger, Simba says to Nala, "You're starting to sound like my father."

She responds, "Good, somebody needs to."

Now, reinforcing his guilt and conviction, Simba says, "I can't go back (and face his fears while trying to help the people of his homeland). It wouldn't change anything anyway. You can't change the past."

All of us can relate to that to some degree. We feel we can't change our past, but our simple acquiescing to it robs us of our future and limits our lives.

Simba turns and runs from Nala and his destiny. Crossing over a body of water, he sees his reflection, but he doesn't like what he sees. As he continues on his pilgrimage, he runs into Rafiki, the High Priest of the jungle. His eccentric ways irritate Simba, but ultimately Simba asks, "Who are you?"

Rafiki responds, "The real question is, 'Who are *you?*'"

Simba comes to a poignant moment in his life as he states, "I thought I knew. Now, I'm not so sure."

Further dialogue with Rafiki causes Simba to state, "I think you're a little confused."

Rafiki responds, "I'm not the one who is confused. You don't even know who you are. You're Mufasa's boy" (in essence, you are the son of a king).

One of the greatest deterrents to breaking the shackles of mediocrity is our failure to realize that God has transformed us into a new creation. Instead, we try to live our lives out of an old identity. You are a completely new creation, but you try to express it through what the apostle Paul calls the "old man."

In his breakthrough book *Wild at Heart*, John Eldredge uses a profound quote from Ireneus, "The glory of God is man fully alive." The truth is, most of us don't feel fully alive. We hate the fact that there seems to be a significant gap between what we know is God's abundant life and the limitations we are presently experiencing.

Now comes the pivotal moment of this encounter for Simba. Rafiki says, "Your father, the king, is still alive." Dazed, confused, but inquisitive, Simba chases after him in pursuit of truth. He comes to the edge of his new adopted country, glances back at it, and turns to continue his pursuit.

The fact for every one of us is that we must decide between the safe, secure, predictable comfort zone we have chosen, or step into the frightening, wild, untamed world of our destiny.

As the chase continues, Rafiki leads Simba to a body of water and exhorts him to look into it. Hesitatingly, Simba gazes into it and steps back, shaking his head. Disappointed, he says, "That's just my reflection (image)."

Insistent, Rafiki chides, "Look harder…you see, he (the father king) lives in you."

How easy it is to forget who it is that lives in us. It is impossible to fail in His will.

As Simba looks the second time, he sees Mufasa's image mingled with his own. Suddenly, a heavenly vision of Mufasa appears and speaks the words of Simba's destiny, and yours.

"Simba, you have forgotten me."

Simba responds, "No, Father, I have not forgotten…."

How easy does it seem that we forget who God is and who we are in Him.

Mufasa continues, "You have forgotten who you are (so you've forgotten me). You are more than you have become."

Simba protests, "I'm not what I used to be."

Finally, Mufasa echoes, "Remember who you are. Remember who you are."

Isn't it amazing as believers how often we forget who we really are?

We allow our past to rob us of our future. Our past disappointments, rejections, bad habits, comfort zones, and attitudes dictate what we will or will not go after. So often they create self-sabotaging behaviors that keep us in line with a depleted self-image.

Finally, Simba emerges from the vision and says to Rafiki, "Looks like the winds are changing. I'm going back to face my past. I've been running from it so long."

In a moment's notice, *whack,* Rafiki hits him in the head with his staff. "What's that for?" Simba cries out.

Rafiki says, "It doesn't matter; it's in the past."

If we could only get that revelation in our hearts. It doesn't really matter; it's in the past. Your past is not a determinant of your future…unless you allow it to be (Philippians 3:12).

Finally, Simba says, "Yeah, but the past still hurts."

The past only has significance according to the value you put on it. The way to change your future is to put a new value on it.

Rafiki says, "There are two things you can do with your past. You can run from it, or learn from it."

Suddenly, Rafiki swings his staff at Simba's head a second time, but Simba ducks and he misses…. Simba had learned from his past. The scene ends with Simba returning to his home in Pride Rock to take his rightful position, no longer fearing his past. While the story has a few New Age implications, the lesson of self-image (God-image) is undeniable.

Unwittingly, this portrays our story as well. Our past poses a daunting image that seeks to intimidate us from moving out of our comfort zones and into the adventurous world of our eternal destiny. This is how social environment seeks to hold us captive.

The movie *Rudy* is a great example of someone who decides to go after his dream to attend and play football at Notre Dame. Unfortunately, he doesn't have the resources or the talent to do either. His dad discourages his idealism by saying something like, "This is our 'lot in life.' I worked in this factory, my dad worked in this factory, and his dad before him. This is what you need to do as well."

Somehow Rudy overcame every obstacle, shortcoming, and self-limitation. He "walks on" the football team and is a part of the Scout Team Squad (practice team). Though he lacks the talent, he makes up for what he lacks in desire. He wins the hearts of his teammates, who convince the coach to let him dress for the last game of his senior year. They prevail on the coach to put Rudy in as the clock is winding down in the last seconds of a win. The coach inserts Rudy for the last play of the game, thus fulfilling his improbable dream of playing football for Notre Dame, with his doubting father and siblings looking on from the stands.

Why do some people overcome obstacles while the vast majority of people allow difficulties to quench the desires of their hearts? It comes back to this element of self-limiting beliefs.

In this first area of social environment, certain backgrounds keep people immobilized in their comfort zones. How many times have you seen someone whose background is one of poverty who willingly accepts the same as his "lot in life"? They receive as their set-point the very standard they've been used to.

I've watched countless times where an over-demanding parent over-disciplines a child and implants a seed of rebellion in them. Rebellion toward parents spills over to rebellion to authority figures and even to God. They never seem to get ahead and wonder why. They can't even see their rebellious attitude, yet it repeatedly sabotages their every promotion in life.

Sometimes the neglect from key figures in your life can breed a mentality of "I'm not worthy of attention from anyone, including God." Perhaps, the opposite takes place. You receive plenty of attention, but it's the wrong kind. Someone is always pointing out your mistakes and shortcomings, saying, "You're not talented enough." Or, "You'll never measure up." That was the issue I dealt with in my own life (chapter 2) when a significant other told me I would never amount to anything. This image prompted self-sabotaging actions that kept me bound to this false image for years. Psychologists suggest that 85 percent of our actions are based on our expectations. My expectation of not amounting to anything caused me momentarily to not step out and try to excel.

The impact of social environment can be easily seen in what transpires in special encounter events when people's lives are legitimately touched. How many times have you seen a person's life dramatically altered at a retreat or a revival, but once they return to their social environment, they go back to their old lifestyle? Why? The image of their social environment is larger than the image of their new encounter.

I once dealt with a young man who said to me over and over, "Why should I try in school? I'm going to fail anyway." We discovered he did have a learning disability. We also learned he was more of a kinetic learner (hands-on), as opposed to an auditory learner. We put this young man on a regiment of "meditation" of love and righteousness. Combining this with putting him in a new learning environment, he has begun to thrive. Failure can be averted and success can be attracted.

AREA #2
AUTHORITY FIGURES

You tend to become what the most important figures in your life think you'll become. What authority figures think about themselves is often projected upon those they have influence over. This is why one of the most important things you can do is to discern who the primary sources of this programming or conditioning in your life were. For most of us, the list will include parents, teachers, friends, coaches, clergy, media, and our culture. Often their training becomes the programming that creates the automatic response system that conditions how we view our world. Our ideas about our abilities, self-worth, and self-image are the product of their reflection. Our attitudes about life and ourselves develop as we interact with key authority figures.

Most psychologists link feelings of low self-esteem and feelings of "I can't" to lifestyles of conditional love.[11] Conditional love, as opposed to unconditional love, is the idea of "love if." I love you *if* you perform in an acceptable manner. This action produces an excessive desire for the approval of others. Ultimately, for many people, it creates inhibition to step out and try unless there's a guarantee of approval. Often a child "learns" to be inhibited and fearful.

Conditional love creates attitudes. An attitude is a mental conditioning that determines our interpretation and response to environment. Attitude is the integration of our self-image (how we see ourselves), self-esteem (how we feel about ourselves), self-worth (how we value ourselves), and the ideal self (the self we want to become). Attitude is the manifestation of who we think we are. *We are not what we think; but rather what we think, we are.*

This is why the projection of what authority figures think can be so devastating. Their selfishness can leave you with a feeling of neglect, which you feel you must deserve. When they hurt you, you often feel the need to hurt. When you're abused, you often feel deserving rather than the victim, or you become an abuser yourself. Failure in your environment by authority figures can perpetuate a mentality and habits of failure in your life. That's why many psychologists will say the greatest determinant of having a good home is if you came from one. Escapism is often the product of our excuse-filled life to protect ourselves from the fear of failure. That's why George Washington Carver stated, "Ninety-nine percent of failure comes from people who have a habit of making excuses."

How an authority figure can have influence on someone can be seen in something I witnessed as a young boy when I tried out for baseball one year. The coach went around and asked everyone what position they played. He came to the young boy next to me, and the boy blurted out, "Batter." His answer was an immediate reflection of what he didn't know. There is no position of batter. You play a defensive position, and batting is your offensive contribution. He simply wanted to play baseball, probably to fit in, and the one thing he knew was that batting produced the glory.

The tryout quickly revealed that this young boy had no baseball skills at all. I watched as he was humiliated and saw the devastating effects it had on his self-esteem in front of the other boys. He withdrew into the "safety" of trying to receive acceptance in any way he could, until finally he simply turned and walked away feeling dejected.

Experiences in life will show what you are good at or not good at. Everyone is not made to be good at everything. Failure at one thing is only an indication that what you're good at has been narrowed down. Will Rogers said it this way: "Everybody's ignorant, just on different topics." Anything that happens to you only has the value you place on it. Joel Osteen, in his book *Your Best Life Now,* tells another story that illustrates how we have to find our strengths as well as our weaknesses.

A little boy went out in the backyard to play with a baseball bat and ball. He declared, "I'm the best hitter in the world," as he threw the ball up into the air to swing and hit it. As the ball spiraled downward, the young boy swung and missed.

Undaunted, he tossed the ball into the air again and similarly confessed, "I'm the best hitter in the world." He swung and missed, for strike two. Now, concentrating more intensely and with determination, he again declared, "I'm the best hitter in the world." *Whoosh.* Again, he swung and missed for strike three. The little boy stepped back and thought for a moment and said, "Well, what do you know, I'm the best pitcher in the world!"[12]

Now, that is what I call an attitude. The right attitude will allow you to put events and proclamations in their proper perspective. How you see yourself makes all the difference in the world.

AREA #3
SELF-IMAGE

We've already defined self-image in this book, but for the sake of emphasis, let me restate it again. Self-image is a predetermined belief of what we can become. It is how we see ourselves. You don't see things as *they* are. You see things as *you* are. This determines how we respond to others, and how others will respond to us. Self-image is what is stored in our subconscious mind (Matthew 12:35-36). Our lives are predominantly determined by this internal picture. This picture controls how we perceive things. It sends a message to our emotional system, physiological system, and neurological system to keep us aligned with our self-image. When the subconscious mind determines we are not on target with our self-image, it will cause a stimulus or suppression of energy, ideas, or activities.[13]

That is why you cannot change a habit until you change your image. You cannot rise above the image you have of yourself in your heart. Your convictions will regulate your thoughts about yourself and your world.

Self-image is the dominant source of your actions and your response to your environment.

Some experts say the greatest psychological discovery of the twentieth century is the discovery of self-worth. The more you value yourself (and as a result, others), the more willing you are to take risks and face obstacles (even failure). According to Maxwell Maltz's breakthrough work, self-image is the key to all human personality and behavior. It is what sets the boundaries of individual accomplishments.[14] Once an idea or belief goes into this picture, it becomes "true" as far as we are personally concerned.[15] In short, we act like the person we conceive ourselves to be. Self-esteem essentially is the summation of all things.

AREA #4
REPETITIOUS INFORMATION

I once heard a speaker quote Adolf Hitler as saying, "If you can tell a lie often enough, people will believe it." How true this seems to be. Recently, while watching the debates for a presidential party, I watched what appeared to be a common agenda to criticize the sitting President. Because the President had no access into the foray, his poll numbers steadily declined. Repetitious display of "fact" (right or wrong) swayed the beliefs of the public.

This is also a dominant principle for advertisers. Marketers say that a person who is about to make a purchase doesn't usually do so until they've seen three ads or commercials. Ads are a combination of information and imagination. *Principles don't change a person; images do.* Repeated exposure to "truth" is convincing people and causing them to move toward certain ends. We've all seen the TV commercials that portray a car with a certain image. The next thing you know, you see the latest model cruising down the street, and heads turn to see it. Finally, you see a shot of the car going down the highway from the driver's perspective…as though you're driving the vehicle. The combination of information plus imagination plus repetition = a need to purchase. Repetitious information, positive or negative, can have a major influence on what we believe. That's why people who hear things over and over tend to accept them as truth. You may hear things like, "When you get older, you get arthritis." The first sign of arthritis is stiffness, so at the first sign of stiffness you think "I must have arthritis." Sure enough, your subconscious mind begins to work to bring it to pass. False repetitious information can be damaging.

AREA #5
EXPERIENCE

This area really is the largest contributor to a person's beliefs. People have a tendency to believe what they experience as being true, without realizing there were contributing factors to the experience. As I stated earlier, all children are born without fear and have spontaneous resolve. All fear is learned by discouraging experiences or conditional love. The good news is that what is learned can be unlearned. Josh Billings once said, "It's not what man knows that hurts him; it's what he knows isn't true" (or at least thinks so). Learning and unlearning both come the same way: repetitious experience. That's why Maxwell Maltz says, "To experience something, you must creatively respond to information."[14] Such action creates patterns in your brain that prompt belief and action.

The two most destructive emotions are fear and discouragement. To "dis"-courage (against courage) costs people the benefit of trying. When a person loses hope, they lose the most powerful motivator to success.[16]

All children are born with an incredible capacity for courage, hope, and risk-taking. I'll never forget when my first child learned how to walk at about eleven or twelve months old. He was in our living room pulling himself up on the furniture and doing his drunken sailor imitation. While he was wobbling and trying to gain his balance, I bounded across the room, beckoning him to come to Daddy. As I said, "Come to Daddy," he looked straight at me, lifted his leg, and for some unknown reason it went sideways, and he fell. It made no difference to him; he simply got up and tried again. He had a complete capacity for hope, resiliency, and success.

People start out as creatures of hope and courage. Experiences, wrongly interpreted, create self-limiting beliefs and often paralyzing fears. Proverbs 13:12 states, "Hope deferred makes the heart sick." Hope unrealized causes the soul to be in conflict with the spirit and saps a person of their resolve. As a newborn child, you were completely unafraid and spontaneous. You laughed, cried, slept, and ate with little or no thought whether anyone approved or disapproved. Somewhere in childhood you learned negative responses to habits, and as a result, you began to demonstrate inhibited and reserved behavior.

The biggest inhibitor is fear. It is most often manifested in the fear of failure or the fear of rejection. Childhood correction without corresponding approval often results in feelings of "I can't" or "I'm not good enough." The fear of rejection is often a result of conditional love in childhood. It is acceptance based on behavior. The result is hypersensitivity to the opinions of others. The results are often paralyzing when it comes to stepping into the destiny God has for you.

OVERCOMING SELF-LIMITING BELIEFS

The key to understanding how to break the bond of mediocrity is not to *run from* self-limiting beliefs (mediocrity), but to *learn from* them. I will include an exercise at the end of this chapter to help you identify self-limiting beliefs.

So, what are the steps to help people identify the self-limiting beliefs that hold them back from experiencing all God has for them?

Identification—Use the exercise at the end of this chapter to identify your set-points, or self-limiting beliefs.

Disassociate yourself from self-limiting beliefs. See yourself differently from what you are conditioned to do or be. This is the part of the imagination in the process of biblical meditation. See Jesus coming into the situation and changing it.

Apply the antidote of God's truth. Once you've identified the set-point, disassociate yourself from it. See yourself in accordance with the truth. "Take" the antidote to your self-limitation. (See my *Barrier Buster's Manual* for a complete list of self-limiting beliefs and their antidotes. This manual also contains lists of scriptures, confessions, applications, and new images in the Lord.) It is here that you take the scriptures of your antidote then turn them into confessions, application, and new images. Once it is done repetitively, any self-limitation is easily broken.

Employ new empowering beliefs. Act on what you now know to be true.

All these steps are to be done within the context of the five steps to biblical meditation given in chapter 3.

God created you to dominate your environment, not to be dominated by it (Genesis 1:26-28). By correcting self-limiting beliefs with the real truth, you can automatically leap to a new level. God made you for abundance. It is now time to live in it.

Why are these five elements of your personal belief system necessary and important? It is because these beliefs formulate an automatic response system from your subconscious mind. The subconscious mind is where your personal belief system resides, and this is where 90 to 95 percent of decisions are made daily. Perhaps you grew up with a parent who imparted ideas to you such as: "Do you think money grows on trees?" "Do you think there's a money tree in the backyard?" "We can't afford this." "There's just not enough to go around." With constant negative repetitious information, the idea that "There's really not enough" gets into your heart (subconscious mind) and formulates the beliefs of lack and decrease. Even though the Word (the truth) says, "Give and it will be given to you" (Luke 6:38), the idea "There's really not enough" has created an automatic response that suggests giving to God results in greater lack. This is why the latest figures of the number of tithers in the church are around 6 to 8 percent.[17]

Many people never actualize (attract) their destiny (Promised Land, in Numbers 14), because they see the "giants" of lack, rejection, fear, and anxiety waiting for them. They "seem like grasshoppers" in their own eyes. Their personal belief system (the subconscious mind chamber of the heart) has already established an automatic response to the obstacles in their path. As a result, they don't enter into God's system (kingdom of God). Therefore, life dictates to them, instead of them dictating to life.

Once you know the sources of your self-limiting thinking, you can look at them through a new mirror (the Word of God to the conscious mind) to establish new truth. Then, through *revelation* from the Holy Spirit and *repetition,* you will recognize people, ideas, and resources that are being attracted to you by the Holy Spirit from God's kingdom. With a new self-image based on God's truth, your new expectation will allow you to step out to do things, make a plan, or take a course of action (in cooperation with the Holy Spirit) to make things come to pass in God's plan for your life.

The exercise at the end of this chapter is not to reinforce negative feelings, but to show you a source of thinking that seeks to keep barriers in your life. This is the hour to destroy your limitations. Remember, self-limiting beliefs are who you *were, not* who you *are!* Remember *who you are!* (2 Corinthians 5:17).

FIVE CHARACTERISTICS OF YOUR PERSONAL BELIEF SYSTEM

Environment

Are there certain settings that remind you of experiences that left you with negative, limiting, or discouraging feelings? _____

_____

_____

_____

_____

Were there certain things in your background that made you think you were dumb, unloved, a failure, or not as good as others? _____

_____

_____

_____

_____

Was there an environment in your home, school, church, or a prominent setting that made you feel self-defeated, worthless, limited, or dumb? _____

_____

_____

_____

Was there an event in your life or family that scared you? _____

_____

_____

_____

_____

Authority Figures

Was there something done to you that makes you feel abused or hurt?

_____
_____
_____

Has an important figure in your life said or done something to you that would make you feel limited, worthless, or willing to settle for what you've always had? _____

_____
_____
_____

Has there ever been an incident with your father that has changed the way you see God? _____

_____
_____
_____

Have there been behavioral or health problems that have become patterns in your family? _____

_____
_____
_____

When you think of certain people who wronged you, do you feel something wrong in the pit of your stomach? _____

_____
_____
_____

Are you able to receive compliments or gifts from others without feeling unworthy or guilty? If no, why? _____

_____

_____

_____

Are there beliefs you have that have come from people in your life
that are contrary to the Word of God?_____

_____

_____

_____

Self-Image

What is the thing you most dislike about yourself? _____

_____

_____

_____

Do you have feelings of being unworthy, unloved, discouraged,
depressed, a failure, anxious, quitting (regularly), wavering in
thought, selfish, prideful, or out of control (anger, lust)? _____

_____

_____

_____

_____

Do you consistently feel stressed?_____

_____

_____

_____

Do you have regular feelings of guilt, grief, worry, rage, or unforgiveness?_____

_____

_____

_____

Repetitious Information

What have you been taught from school, home, friends, work, media, teachers, or coaches that is contrary to the Word of God? _____

_____

_____

_____

_____

What things have been reinforced in you that may be construed as limiting?_____

_____

_____

_____

Experience

What experience have you had that was beyond your control, and left you feeling fearful, negative, or alone? _____

_____

_____

_____

What happened to you that you would consider your biggest test in life? What is your reflection on it? _____

_____

_____

_____

What failure in your life looms large in your memory? _____

_____

_____

_____

What regret do you have in life? _____

_____

_____

_____

_____

What is the one thing you wish never had happened to you? _____

_____

_____

_____

_____

What happened in your childhood, teenage years, or college years you wish hadn't? _____

_____

_____

_____

_____

_____

KEYS

You can never rise above the image you have of yourself in your heart.

Many times, self-limiting beliefs are the product of five areas in your life: (1) social environment, (2) authority figures, (3) self-image, (4) repetitious information, and (5) experience.

Once you determine self-limiting beliefs, refuse to accept the limitations of the world's system.

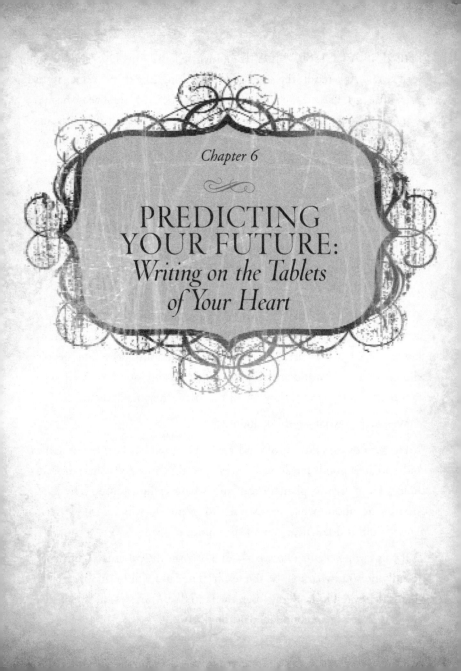

Chapter 6

PREDICTING
YOUR FUTURE:
*Writing on the Tablets
of Your Heart*

THERE IS A CLASSIC MOVIE moment when Doris Day sings "Que Será, Será." As I recall, the song goes something like this: "When I was just a little girl, I asked my mother, what will I be?… Here's what she said to me. 'Que Será, Será. Whatever will be, will be. The future's not ours to see. Que Será, Será.'" What nonsense! Though that might be a memorable song in a famous musical, it is totally contrary to biblical truth on how to approach life.

This passive mentality embraces drifting along in life and taking whatever comes your way. This is hardly the intent of Scripture (see Matthew 11:12). That's why business guru Peter Drucker once said in a Tulsa seminar I attended, "The best way to predict your future is to create it."

George Bernard Shaw, in Earl Nightengale's book, *The Strangest Secret,* is quoted as saying, "People are always blaming their circumstances for what they are. I don't believe in circumstances. The people who get on in this world are people who get up and look for the circumstances they want, and if they can't find them, they make them."

We become what we think about.

He goes on to add a profound analogy: suppose a farmer has some land and it is good, fertile soil. In essence the land gives the farmer a choice. He is free to plant in the land whatever he chooses. The land doesn't care about what he chooses to plant. It will return what is planted, and it doesn't care about the choice of seed.

If this farmer plants two seeds—one is corn, the other is nightshade, a deadly poison, what will be the result? The land will invariably return what is deposited in it. Remember, the land doesn't care what is planted. Its job is to create an abundance of the deposit.

The human mind is far more fertile and mysterious than any land, but it works the same way. It doesn't care what we plant—success or failure—its job is to yield increase. What we plant will return to us.[1]

Jesus said that He came to give you life and life more abundantly" (John 10:10). In other words, He has come to give you life as a super-achiever, and yet those fulfilling this seem to be few and far between. God's purpose for you is that you find the life you were born to live, fulfill your destiny, and live in success and prosperity. You need to settle this issue in you. You must discover your value, operate in the laws of God, and manifest His kingdom wherever you go.

The kingdom of heaven is not simply an eternal destiny as much as it is a manner of rule, governance, or system.[2] It is a system based on God's laws. A law is a principle that tells you how a thing works best. In this case, the "thing" is the kingdom of God. Once these laws are mastered, in connection to the kingdom, you know how the manifestations of abundance will come into your life.

The goal of this book is to create a systematic plan to transform your personal belief system, not based on reflection from an improper social environment, incorrect authority figures, a poor self-image, false repetitious information, or bad experiences, but solely based on the truth of God's immutable Word.

What I think determines what I believe. What I believe determines my decisions. My decisions determine what I can accomplish. The results are a matter of choice (Deuteronomy 30:19). Renewing my mind, establishing my heart, and transforming my personal belief system is not simply memorizing scripture (truth). It is the transformation of my decision-making.

God's plan and purpose for you *is* productivity at every level. John states in 3 John 2, "Beloved, I wish above all things that you may prosper and be in health, even as thy soul prospereth" (KJV). Notice it is an aberration in the kingdom's system to be in sickness and poverty. The manifestation, however, is not automatic. It is dependent on a prosperous soul. What is a prosperous soul? A prosperous soul is a renewed mind, a persuaded, submitted will, positive emotions, and a focused imagination (meditation). These things, in turn, produce health and prosperity.

So, why is it so many people have difficulty manifesting this promise? Paul deals with this in Ephesians 4:17. He states, "So I tell you this, and insist on it in the Lord, that you must no longer live as the Gentiles do (people who are out of habit with God's thinking)[3] in the futility of their thinking." What is this? It is the world's system. This system can create a feeling of being untrustworthy, worthless, or incapable of receiving a desired end from God.

He goes on to say, "They are darkened (un-illuminated) in their understanding and separated from the life of God…" (Ephesians 4:18). The very things you want God to manifest, you cannot manifest because you're thinking according to the wrong system and are separated from the Source of your true supply.

Paul adds, "…because of the ignorance that is in them due to the hardening of their hearts" (Ephesians 4:18). The hardening of your heart is when you are more sensitive to the natural than you are to the supernatural (see Mark 6:45-52; 8:1-21). There is no alignment or congruency in your heart.

Here's the result: "Having lost all sensitivity (to God), they have given themselves over to sensuality" (Ephesians 4:19). Sensuality is always a substitute for sensitivity. Sensuality is an act of the flesh. Flesh is man's attempt to do God's will his own way (see Romans 8:5). Once God sees that characteristic, He backs off and lets people try to meet their needs by natural means until they come to the end of themselves. And then some, not all, turn to Him and learn to drink from the cistern of living water that never runs dry.

He continues, "...so as to indulge in every kind of impurity..." (Ephesians 4:19). What is impurity? It's not just unacceptable behavior. Impurity really means mixture. If another substance is mixed with gold, the gold is impure. Most Christians live their lives as mixture. They mix the old man with their new identity, which hinders them from living life to the fullest. God made you a new creation, with truth and grace (God's ability) to manifest His resources of His kingdom. The mixture (allowing impurities in your life) dilutes your effectiveness and true productivity.

Paul concludes the section in Ephesians with the answer, "To be made new in the attitude of your minds; and put on the new self, created to be like God in true righteousness and holiness" (Ephesians 4:23, 24). What a remarkable revelation. As a believer, we are to put on the new self and understand who we have become as a new creature. *See* yourself according to the truth. "Be made new in the attitude of your mind." Remember, the term *attitude* means "mental conditioning that determines our interpretation or response to our environment." It is the integration of our self-image, self-esteem, self-worth, and ideal self. Self-image is how you see yourself. Self-worth is how you value yourself. Self-esteem is how you feel about yourself. The ideal self is the person you see yourself becoming. It is the way you see yourself, and you will act according to that image. What Paul is saying is this: if you see yourself differently, then the truth will change your viewpoint—it's reality. Then, act in accordance to truth.

IT'S ALL ABOUT ATTITUDE

I love the little story that has been told by a number of motivational speakers about the two shoe salesmen. The story goes like this. Two salesmen from competing companies traveled to Africa to explore the shoe market. The first salesman hated the assignment and abhorred his mission. The second salesman was excited about the opportunity and viewed it as a great chance for advancement in the company.

When they arrived in the African country, they studied the local market for shoes. After gathering the information they needed, they both sent telegrams to the home office with their observations. The first salesman, who didn't want to be there, wrote, "The time here has been wasted. There is no market for shoes in this country. No one here wears shoes." The second salesman, who saw this venture from a different perspective, wrote this, "Incredible trip! This is a market of unlimited opportunity. No one here wears shoes."[4]

The point is, you see what you already believe.[5] You do not believe what you see; you see what you already believe. You view your life (world) through the lens of beliefs, attitudes, prejudices, and preconceived notions. You are not what you think; what you *think,* you *are.*[6] This is why Josh Billings' quote is so important: "It is not what we don't know that prevents us from succeeding. It's what we know just ain't so, is our greatest obstacle." The greatest secret of God's kingdom is as much about unlearning as well as learning to see the truth of who you really are. You must recognize your present beliefs are responsible for where you are right now in life. God's secret is to break those beliefs and show you how to live by His kingdom laws. There is a marketing principle by Henry Beckwith that says, "People hear what they see."[7] You can tell them anything, but they have a tendency to believe what they see. That's why when you tell people that God wants to prosper them, people immediately look to see if they can find any prosperity around them.

The job of the conscious mind is to determine truth. The job of the subconscious mind is to take whatever the conscious mind determines is true and create an automatic response system to carry it out. That's why perceived truth always battles new truths. Your subconscious mind will automatically make decisions in agreement with established truth—right or wrong. Your personal belief system is stronger than anything I can say to you. Knowing this is a major key when your subconscious mind is in opposition to God's truth.

Your dominant thoughts get into your heart, and whatever is in your heart, that's what you are going to do. This is the "missing ingredient" to real productivity and "transformation" in your life. What is learned can be unlearned, so that new beliefs can replace the false ones that have been lodged in your heart. These new beliefs will change your personal belief system, which will now consist of a renewed mind, an established heart, and increased faith. Renewed thinking done consistently creates dominant thoughts that get into your heart. When you have an established heart, it creates corresponding actions, and these consistent actions increase faith. Increased faith brings increased manifestations.

WRITING ON THE TABLETS OF YOUR HEART

Everything that happens in your life comes out of your heart. If you want to break the pattern of your present and predict your future, you must learn to write on the tablets of your heart. Look at this principle in Proverbs 7:1-3: "My son, keep my words and store up my commands within you. Keep my commands and you will live; guard my teachings as the apple of your eye. Bind them on your fingers; write them on the tablets of your heart."

The following are *five key principles* to help you to write on your heart God's truth and thereby predict your own future:

1. *Store commands in your inner man (within you).* This term *store* means "to put aside a supply for use when needed."[8] Therefore, I take the truth of God's Word and store it in my heart and mind

until I have future need of it. I do this by study and meditation (all five steps). Meditation is a combination of information and emotion. Remember, God dwells in your spirit by salvation, but He dwells in your heart by faith (Ephesians 3:16, 17). Faith is believing the truth of a renewed mind, an established heart, and a new image on the inside of you.

2. *Keep my commands.* The term *keep* means "to guard or protect."[9] I protect what I store through the act of thanksgiving (see Philippians 4:6, 7). Thanksgiving puts a guard over my heart and mind. Thanksgiving is a powerful force. Emotions travel 80,000 times faster than a thought. Emotions, like thanksgiving, cause your will and your mind to move into action toward a goal. That is why God's Word mixed with thanksgiving protects the truth in your heart and mind. It helps line the mind up to God's truth and, in turn, line up with your spirit. It is here that the power of God is released.

Since the subconscious mind doesn't recognize positives or negatives, or real or imagined, it recognizes the emotion as an indication of the establishment of truth and rallies toward that end. That is why thanksgiving is such a powerful force.

The writer in Proverbs 7 says, if you do this, you will live. This doesn't mean you'll exist or that God will "snuff you out" if you don't. It means you will have the vitality (or abundance) for which you were created. The shackles of lack or mediocrity will be broken from your life.

3. *Guard my teachings as the apple of your eye.* In other words, watch over this process because this is the most important thing you can do. Your diligence in this effort indicates its value to you. Don't let new circumstances rob you of God's newly established truth. Do something daily toward your highest priority.

4. *Bind them on your fingers.* The old idea of tying a string around your finger to remind you of something is the idea here. It's like George Bailey's uncle in the movie *It's a Wonderful Life*. He was always trying to remind himself of something by tying a string on his finger. This idea is to remind yourself of something through recognition. When recognition of a new truth is done repetitively it promotes perception of a new truth. It takes twenty-one days (some experts say thirty days, or slightly more) to create a new habit. Let repetition help you see new truths (images) in your life.

5. *Write them on the tablets of your heart.* In other words, storing (meditation), keeping (protecting), guarding (prioritizing), and binding (repetition) all contribute to writing on the tablets of my heart. Once it's in my heart, it will dictate my actions.

   Writing on the tablets of our heart is primarily influencing the soul chamber and, in particular, the subconscious mind. This is the part of our heart that tries to make what we believe come to pass. This is where your personal belief system creates an automatic response system that presupposes your actions. This is why you do what you really believe. This is why writing on the tablets of your heart is far more than scripture memorization. You must take the three P's to imprint something on your heart. You must make new truth personal, positive, and present tense.

   To imprint new truth you want to incorporate into your heart, you must take the "you" of the new truth and make it "I", or "my," or "me." For instance, if you are meditating on Psalm 35:27 (Amplified Bible), "Let the Lord be magnified, Who takes pleasure in the prosperity of His servant," make the new truth you want to incorporate into your heart personal. "Lord, I thank You that You delight in my prosperity. I rejoice that You delight in and are excited about prospering me." It must also be positive. Don't think about overcoming your present lack, because focusing on lack causes you to attract lack. Instead, focus on your present prosperity. Don't look at the negative; look at the positive. Finally, make it present tense. "I am" prospering in everything I do. Get specific about a present situation you're involved in now. Why? Because, your heart (subconscious mind of the soul) can't tell the difference between what's real and what's imagined. When the subconscious mind is convinced of a truth, it will set in motion what's necessary to bring it to pass. When you focus on God's truth, the Holy Spirit will help you recognize people, ideas, and resources to make your belief become a reality. Let your meditation allow you to see (imagine) this truth in your heart. See the benefits. Ponder the joy of your new reality. See yourself walking out the truth. Imprint it on your heart.

This is further reinforced in Proverbs three. Virtually every believer knows Proverbs 3:5-6: "Trust in the LORD with all your heart and lean not on your own understanding; in all your ways acknowledge him, and he will make your paths straight." It's a powerful verse. But, it is preceded by verses 1-4: "My son, do not forget my teaching, but keep my commands in your heart, for they will prolong your life many years and bring you prosperity. Let love and faithfulness never leave you; bind them around your neck, write them on the tablet of your heart...." Directing our paths is preceded by writing on the tablets of our heart.

He starts out saying, "Do not forget my teaching...." Why? It is because the five elements of your personal belief system (1. social environment, 2. authority figures, 3. self-image, 4. repetitious information, and 5. experience) all have negative happenings that are constantly challenging truth with fact.

Now, again he says, "keep, store, guard, bind, repeat and write on your heart, and you'll gain vitality of life and prosperity." You will be *fully alive*. Once you've mastered these principles, you find yourself not leaning to your past experience as a guide, but instead recognize new truth, and God will allow you to see people, ideas, and resources according to your most dominant thoughts (direct your paths).

I was doing a recent conference in Hawaii in a beautiful setting. I had this sense in me that I was in this setting for a divine purpose. After several days, it still was not apparent to me. I declined my roommate's offer to go "work out" later in the week so that I could pray instead. After two hours of prayer (one in my room, the other by the ocean), God spoke six things to me. The first had to do with an authority figure in my past. The person had a habit of what I call "poor mouthing." People who "poor mouth" have a habit of always seeing and saying the negative side of things. This person not only constantly spoke this way in front of me, but this person modeled this behavior. Suddenly, I realized that this self-limitation had invaded my life in certain arenas.

The moment I realized this, I began to disassociate myself from an improper image. I began to store, keep, protect, guard, and write a new image on my heart of belief and expectation. That moment my new image became absolutely real, and six things leaped out of my heart that I was to do. One of them was to get to talk privately with one of the main speakers at this conference. After some effort to make that a reality, we got together. I began to share some revelations God had placed on my heart. He agreed to open doors in the publishing arena and a couple of other areas. My point is not to accentuate my good fortune of a serendipitous occurrence, but to point out how breaking a set-point from my past created a new image in my heart that opened doors to my future. The result was that God directed my paths.

Paul recalls a similar idea in 2 Corinthians 3:3: "You show that you are a letter from Christ, the result of our ministry, written not with ink but with the Spirit of the living God, not on tablets of stone but on tablets of human hearts." Again, God's design is to imprint His thoughts on your heart. All of a person's faith comes out of a person's heart. We do not accomplish this process by ourselves; it is the product of the Holy Spirit's working in our lives. Paul continues by saying, "Such confidence...is ours, through Christ before God" (2 Corinthians 3:4). The result of a newly imprinted heart is a new image that fills us with true confidence. True confidence is the product of a transformed self-image. This produces righteousness by faith, which allows us to see the reflection of God's work and to be transformed from one level of glory (view and opinion of God, manifestation of His presence[10]) to another (2 Corinthians 3:18).

Ezekiel amplifies on this: "I will give you a new heart and put a new spirit in you; I will remove from you your heart of stone and give you a heart of flesh. And I will put my Spirit in you and move you to follow my decrees and be careful to keep my laws" (36:26, 27). As you transform your heart to God's view and opinion, it becomes easy to keep His laws. The prophet Jeremiah declares, "I will put my laws in their minds and write it on their hearts. I will be their God, and they will be my people" (31:33). Once your heart is changed, believing new truth becomes easy.

HIS YOKE IS BETTER

Most of the time when you answer a question about life, your answer is conditioned by your experience. Experience is anything observed or lived through; all that has happened to a person. It is the reaction to events. It is a person's personal referral system. It is your data bank of all your memories stored in your mind. You generally ask the question, "Does this jive with my experience from the past? Does this correlate with what I know to be true?" When I'm doing a conference, if I make the statement, "Parenting is easy!" I usually get a gasp from the audience. For many people this does not correlate to their experience. They've had quite a different experience, especially if they've had to deal with a rebellious son or daughter. Or, how about this, "Crime doesn't pay." Oh, really, there are many people who have found it to be quite profitable and are living the high life hidden in this country or abroad. How you view life depends on your experience.

So, if I asked the question, "Is Christianity easy?" most believers would protest vociferously. Why? There's no corroboration with their experience. Listen to what Jesus said: "Come to Me, all *you* who labor and are heavy laden, and I will give you rest. Take My yoke upon you and learn from Me, for I am gentle and lowly in heart, and you will find rest for your souls. For My yoke *is* easy and My burden is light" (Matthew 11:28-30).[11] He reveals five amazing keys in this short passage concerning the designed ease of the Christian life:

1. *When you are weary and weak, come to God.* Why is it so many of us are like Simba in the *Lion King?* When we are weak, weary, and messed up, we want to run from God, instead of run to Him. Listen to the writer of Hebrews: "Let us then approach the throne of grace with confidence, so that we may receive mercy and find grace to help us in our time of need" (4:16).

   Notice first, it's a throne of grace, not judgment. The second thing to notice is when do we come? When we are in need. What kind of need is, he referring to? When I'm weary, weak, or when I've messed up. When I've done the thing I said I'd never do. Most of us want to run from God, not to Him. And yet this verse invites us to come to a heavenly Father who longs to help just at the moment we feel weak and failing.

Not are we only to come to Him, but look how we're to come: with confidence. How can I possibly come to God with confidence when I've messed up? We can come with confidence not because of us, but because of the righteousness we have in Jesus. Righteousness is right standing with God, not based on what I've done, but receiving by faith what He has done on my behalf. I couldn't keep the law, so Jesus did it for me. Now I receive it by faith in Him (see Romans 3:20-26; 2 Corinthians 5:20; Romans 10:3, 4; Romans 5:17-19; 1 Corinthians 15:34; Philippians 3:7-11; Matthew 6:32, 33; Psalm 112:3, 6-8; 1 Timothy 1:9). So, even when I mess up, I can come to Him, not run from Him.

2. *Then I will give you rest* (rest correlates to grace, see Hebrews 4:10). This second step correlates again to Hebrews 4:16. When I come to His throne of grace, He gives me mercy and grace to help in time of need. These two words do not mean the same thing. Mercy is God not giving us what we deserve. Grace is God giving us what we don't deserve. It is God's enablement or His ability.[12] Grace is God's ability to do what our ability cannot do. We were not made to follow the patterns of success on our own abilities. We are to get yoked up to Him. Two oxen yoked together share the burden. I can't live the super-abundant, super-achieving lifestyle apart from His infusion of grace (see the last chapter for more detail on how this works).

3. *Learn of me.* We receive the help we need by humbly submitting to God's ways. Now, what are His ways? His ways are His principles and laws of how things are to be done. Humility is not some doormat being willfully trampled upon. It is not some limp wrist nondescript manner of pursuing something. The word *humility* means "to submit to the view and opinion of God."[13] It is not simply some lowly mind-set. Humility says, "If God says I can, I

can. If God says I am, I am. If God says I have, I have."[14] The key is learning God's laws of success. Earlier we shared about the law in physics called the law of entropy, which says "Things left unattended tend toward chaos." How true this law is for us as people. Things left unattended in our lives swing toward the chaotic. Transformation comes from intentionally going after shortcomings and applying God's principles. All change for God is intentional, not haphazard. It comes from learning His ways.

4. *For I am…humble of heart,* means that your heart is submitted to the view and opinion of God. Your soul is submitted to your spirit in your heart by the renewing of your mind.

The result is that you will find rest or grace (God's ability on your behalf) for your heart and your soul. Obeying His ways produces a yoke that is easy and light (Matthew 11:30). The Christian life becomes easy and vigorous because we are doing it in His strength and not ours.

There are two ways you can tell if a revelation is in your heart: (1) It changes your image of yourself in that area, and (2) that area becomes easy.[15] Any lasting change begins by changing the image of yourself in that area. That is the biggest part of what biblical meditation does in your life. It is amazing to me how easy certain things are in my life now. For instance, I'm never tempted to do drugs. Why? The right image of obeying God in that area is already in my heart. My past is filled with experiences with alcohol, but today I'm never tempted with alcohol. Why? My view and opinion of my heart are submitted to God's principles. It's easy and light.

FOUR STEPS TO REST AND GRACE

There are *four basic steps to transformation* in any area of your life:

Identification—Identify your set-point. (Go back to chapter 5.) Examine the five areas of your personal belief system. Where are your set-points and self-limiting beliefs?

Disassociation—Use your meditation to disassociate yourself from the image of that set-point. See God changing the situation in your heart.

Apply the antidote—Focus on the truth, not just the facts. Truth is always stronger than fact. You might be struggling with lack, but "God delights in the prosperity of His servants."[16] Repetitiously reinforce the truth.

Employ new empowering beliefs—Through confession and applying the truth, watch a remarkable turnaround take place.

I was working with a dynamic young woman, but because of a deprecating past experience, she found herself on a roller coaster with her emotions. One day she was up, and the next she was in the depths of depression. Frankly, there was very little stability in her life, so I took her through these four steps.

First, I asked her not to ignore her past hurt, but to focus and see it clearly. I even asked her to identify the intensity of how she felt. Next, I asked her to disassociate herself from the false guilt she was experiencing from this memory. I told her to meditate on righteousness and love, while seeing Jesus healing this tragic memory. As she applied the antidote of love and righteousness to her life, I watched an amazing transformation take place. Overwhelming confidence poured into her life, and she began to walk in unbridled expectation. Daily she began to employ her newfound image and beliefs. Almost overnight she started recognizing people, ideas, and resources she had been missing. Every area of her life started moving in a new direction. The transformation was as startling as the story of the woman with amnesia. Today she is a successful business woman who is fulfilled in her life.

How do you employ new empowering beliefs? Once revelation starts to get down in your heart, you've got to make them work for you. How? Every day do something to reinforce your highest priority. Find something to do that reinforces your new belief system. If you are "believing" God for new living quarters, drive by an area where you would like to live and just dream. If you want to lose weight, go window shopping for your new size. Begin to act in accordance to your new beliefs. Also, reinforce and reward your progress. If you want to lose fifty pounds, but you've lost twenty pounds, reward yourself (in this case, don't do it with food). Go shopping or get a massage or some activity that you enjoy.

Remember, some failure is inevitable. You may experience a set-back or two. Your attitude when you fail will make all the difference in the world. Thomas Edison is credited as being the greatest inventor of our time. He is credited with 1,093 patents. It is also true that Edison was also the greatest "failure" of our time. He failed many more times than he had breakthroughs. He would experiment and fail over and over again. His attitude was simply this: success is inevitable and failure is not an option. It is said that Edison's response to failure was, "I knew the day would come, when I would run out of ways it would not work." This was after he had tried ten thousand times (failures). Don't let some minor set-back deter you from your destiny. Remember, *failure is merely an opportunity to start again more intelligently.*

Once you master renewing your mind, establishing your heart, and transforming your personal belief system, you will be positioned to learn the laws that make success inevitable. Once biblical meditation secures new empowering beliefs, the momentum to do God's will, will be like a wind to your sails. Now, it's time to examine how to apply the Law of Attraction to productivity in every area of your life.

KEYS

Remember the *five keys to writing on the tablets of your heart:*

1. Store the truth of God's Word in you.

2. Study until you have revelation.

3. Meditate.

4. Let God's truth create a new image in you.

5. Keep, guard, and protect what has been given to you with thanksgiving. Thanksgiving reinforces to the subconscious mind the truth associated with it as something it needs to pursue until what you desire becomes true.

Guard your new truth ("as the apple of your eye") as the most important pursuit of your life. Don't let new current circumstances rob you of the truth.

Build them on your prayers or make their repetition your priority. It takes twenty-one days to create a new habit.

Write them on your heart. Remember, your boundaries in life come out of your heart. By confessing God's truth as personal, present tense, and positive, new truth becomes imprinted on your heart.

In summary:

Identify self-limiting beliefs.

Disassociate yourself from the image of these self-limiting beliefs through the imagination stage of biblical meditation.

Apply the antidote of the truth of the perspective of God's Word.

Employ new empowering beliefs by confessing and applying God's Word.

Chapter 7

THE SECRET'S
SECRET
*Faith: Bringing
Heaven to Earth*

THE REAL QUESTION BECOMES, "How do I use the Law of Attraction to increase my personal productivity?" The Law of Attraction says, "You attract to yourself people, ideas, and resources according to your most dominant thoughts."

In the book *The Secret,* James Ray makes it sound as simple as Aladdin's Lamp. You simply rub the lamp, then a genie appears and says, "Your wish is my command."[1] The genie assumes that all that you think about, you want.[2] Thus, your thinking magically manifests (brings to pass) your desires. The real truth of the matter is your subconscious mind is working to make your dominant thoughts come to pass. Once your mind is renewed to kingdom laws, the Holy Spirit is actively bringing you provision from the kingdom of heaven. So now your renewed mind is able to recognize God's provisions and bring them into manifestation (being). It is not a magic wand, Aladdin's lamp, or pixie dust. Bottom line, you create into reality what you focus on according to God's truth.

If it were as simple as merely thinking about something, most people would be manifesting a multiplicity of things, most for which they wouldn't be ready. The key law to "prove" or "manifest" God's kingdom is "faith." Somehow in the body of Christ, we've reduced this concept to some mysterious enigma that nobody can truly understand. How much faith is necessary to receive God's provision? How do I conjure up enough faith to get "stuff" to work?

Amazingly, *The Secret* made the process simple by outlining the principles found in Mark 11:24:

Ask

Believe

Receive

Mark 11:24 says, "Whatever you *ask* for in prayer, *believe* that you have *received* it, and it will be yours." (emphasis mine). *The Secret* suggests that the moment you ask, believe, and know you have it in the "unseen," the entire universe shifts to bring it into the "seen."[3] The universe, in essence, is mirroring back your dominant thoughts. You are emitting a "feeling frequency" of receiving something, and you attract it unto yourself. Like most "New Thought" or "New Age" thought processes, it has a kernel of truth with just enough poison to make it lethal. The world's system does have elements of productivity, but it will always lack what Joshua calls "good success" (Joshua 1:8). That is prosperity without divorce, or increase without rebellious children, etc. It is God's intent to provide abundance to your life without sorrow.

Indeed, we do attract our dominant renewed thoughts, but not magically from some impersonal universe, gilded in a humanistic virtuoso. This is about faith in a loving personal God whose desire is to bless you from the abundance of His kingdom, both now and in eternity.

To best understand the three-fold set of principles from Mark 11:24, we must understand its context.

THE GOD-KIND OF FAITH

Mark 11:22 says, "…'Have faith in God,' Jesus answered." Many scholars believe this verse is better translated from the Greek in the objective genetive, which means the disciples must go on having trust and complete reliance on God. It is a continual action, a way of life. The idea of the objective genetive gives you the thought that this verse is better translated, "Have the faith *of* God" or the *God-kind of faith*.[4] We use this God-given, God-kind of faith, but we put it in the Lord, not in our actions, ability, or even our faith.[5]

We have been given the God-kind of faith in our lives. Let's look at what that means to us. In Matthew 17:14, we read of the story of a demon-possessed boy. The boy has seizures, is convulsed, and throws himself into the fire or water. In desperation the father cries out to Jesus for help, because His disciples could not heal his son or deliver him from the demon that tormented him.

Jesus rebukes His disciples and replies, "O unbelieving and perverse generation,… how long shall I put up with you? Bring the boy here to me" (v.17).

You can almost hear the frustration in Jesus' response (to what most think is toward His disciples). It's as if He says, "You boys have been with me in church (synagogue) every week (every day), you attended the special healing seminar, you've been to the 'How to win friends and cast out demons retreat, and still you don't get it."

Finally, they bring the boy to Jesus, and He casts out the demon and heals him. Later in a private moment and in a sense of amazement, the disciples ask Jesus,… "Why could we not cast it out?" (Matthew 17:19 NKJV).

Jesus replies, "Because you have so little faith. I tell you the truth, if you have faith as small as a mustard seed, you can say to this mountain, 'Move from here to there,' and it will move. Nothing will be impossible for you" (Matthew 17:20).

For years this verse confused me. On one hand, Jesus says, "Your problem is you have so little faith." On the other hand, He says, "If you have faith as small as a mustard seed…." If you held a mustard seed in your hand, it is so small it is almost imperceptible. This is almost contradictory in concept. When Jesus says it is because you have "so little faith," and then tells them to have faith as "small as a mustard seed," it is difficult to see how the two correlate. The meaning comes across much clearer in the King James Version, which translates the verse better. They couldn't drive it out "because of their (your) unbelief." The problem wasn't their little faith, but their unbelief. The smallest amount of faith will move the obstacle if it is not negated by our unbelief. The challenge most of us face is that our social backgrounds, authority figures, self-image, repetitive information, or our experiences have set up self-limiting beliefs that are contrary to the knowledge of God (2 Corinthians 10:3-6). In other words, your unbelief negates your belief. Most people feel you can only have faith or unbelief, but not both at the same time. This is actually what James calls double-mindedness. The Bible says, "That man should not think he will receive anything from the Lord; he is a double-minded man, unstable in all he does" (James 1:7-8). The problem is not "enough faith." It is faith mixed with unbelief. This is why Jesus told Jairus in Luke 8:50: "Believe only!" (KJV).[6] Believe without the unbelief. Believe without the hindrances of unrenewed, self-limiting beliefs.

The problem is not having enough faith. The Scripture says, "in accordance with *the* measure of faith God has given you" (Romans 12:3, emphasis mine). It doesn't say every man was given "a" measure of faith. There are not different measures dispensed by God. God doesn't give massive faith to one and a little faith to another. We're all given equal faith at salvation. The issue isn't that we don't have enough faith. The faith we do have has been rendered ineffective because we've not renewed our minds to what we already have. All people get the same measure. Peter says it like this, "…to them that have obtained *like precious faith* (2 Peter 1:1, KJV, emphasis mine)." The faith we've received is the same faith Peter used to raise Dorcas from the dead (Acts 9:36). In Galatians 2:20, we are told to live our lives by what Paul calls "the faith *of* the Son of God" (KJV, emphasis mine). Our problem is not having insufficient faith; we simply don't renew our minds to eliminate elements of trace of unbelief. Once we have changed the image in our heart, eliminated elements of unbelief, and believe the truth, then our faith will come alive and be capable of doing what Jesus said in John 14:12: "I tell you the truth, anyone who has faith in me will do what I have been doing. He will do even *greater* things than these, because I am going to the Father."

I can hear the protests already: "The Bible talks about 'no faith,' 'little faith,' and also 'great faith.'" This is not really about how much faith you have, but how much faith you are manifesting. You don't really increase your faith in quantity but quality. You renew your mind to what you already have, and then you simply learn to use it. You cast off unbelief, and your belief begins to operate as it should.

That's a pretty huge paradigm shift in thinking for some people. To say I can't increase my faith is contrary to what we are normally taught. If it helps you to think that you must increase your faith to manifest God's kingdom (because the Bible does speak in several places of varying degrees of faith: Matthew 6:30; 8:10; 14:31, 16:8; 2 Corinthians 10:15, these are more manifestations of faith than an increase of what you already possess), that is fine with me, but it helps me to understand that I presently have everything I need. I only need to learn how to use it more effectively.

You might be thinking then, "Why did the disciples ask to increase their faith (Luke 17:5)?" Jesus responds similarly to what He did in Matthew 17, "If you have faith as small as a mustard seed, you can say to this mulberry tree, 'Be uprooted and planted in the sea,' and it will obey you." Then what follows this thought process seems totally "off the cuff" in verses 7-10. Jesus then talks about the duty of a servant. How does this apply to "increase our faith"? Is He really answering their question? Yes! What He is saying is that faith is like a servant. Servants shouldn't just sit around in leisure; they must do their master's will.[7] This is similar with our "faith." We must learn to use what we already have and do our Lord's will.

A MEASURE OF FAITH VERSUS UNBELIEF

The story in Matthew 17 is a key to understand that you have all the faith you'll ever need, as long as you don't negate it with unbelief. It is like having a heavy object with two ropes attached to it. If you pull it in the same direction, you can move the object. If, however, you pull on the ropes in opposite directions with equal force, the weight remains immobilized.[8] In the same way, unbelief can negate the faith that God has deposited in your life. Self-limiting beliefs can cause you to limp toward your destiny when God wants you to take ever-increasing leaps of faith.

Unbelief or self-limiting beliefs may come from the five areas of your personal belief system, but they originate from a hardened heart. Andrew Womack, in his book *Hardness of Heart,* tells how this occurs. In Mark 6, Jesus has just fed 5,000 people with 5 loaves and 2 fish. He has also just walked on the water to His disciples who were crossing the Sea of Galilee in a boat. In verses 51 and 52 we read, "Then he climbed into the boat with them, and the wind died down. They were completely amazed, for they had not understood about the loaves; their hearts were hardened." The question becomes, "Why were they so amazed that Jesus walked on water?" Obviously, it is an astonishing event. Jesus says that they were amazed because of the "hardness of their hearts." The next verse states, "For they considered not the miracle of the loaves...." The term *considered not* literally means "to take into account, examine, to describe, to meditate on or focus on."[9] Because they didn't meditate or focus on what Jesus had done earlier in the miracle of feeding the 5,000 (perhaps 20,000 with women and children), the passage says that "their hearts were hardened." When I hear somebody elaborate on a "hardened heart," they usually refer to a rebellious heart. But this is not the case with the circumstances surrounding this event. The disciples weren't being rebellious; they were just not sensitive to the meaning of the prior events that had transpired. The term *hardened* means "calloused, blind, or insensitive."[10] What a *hardened heart* means in this context is they were more sensitive to the natural (the "seen") than they were to the supernatural (the "unseen").[11]

The disciples didn't focus on or understand the dynamics of feeding the multitude with five simple loaves and two fish. So, they couldn't make the connection to the miracle of walking on the water. It is so easy to focus more on the natural occurrences. What we focus on is what we tend to create (or manifest). It is easier to focus on what is visible rather than what is invisible.

Let me give you a practical example from my own life. It was my wife Judy's and my privilege to pay for our sons' education. This amounted to a substantial amount, but we felt it was a well-deserved investment. When my middle son graduated from undergraduate school, he decided to take a Graduate Leadership Course in Colorado Springs. He was going to secure the financing to take care of it. He came home during a break about two weeks before his graduation. He said to us during the break, "Oh, by the way, don't forget to be ready to make the payment for graduation next week."

The announcement took us totally off guard. Halfway in panic Judy said to me, "We'll have to take out a loan from the bank."

Without thinking I drove straight to the bank and secured the loan. On the way out of the bank, I heard God say, "Did I tell you to get a loan?"

You can almost hear the meekness in my voice as I replied, "No sir!" Suddenly, I realized what I had done. I had looked to the natural before even considering the supernatural. In obedience I canceled the loan. In one week the money came from a totally unexpected source.

The provision was already there. I simply had to release my faith for it. It was the unseen coming to the seen. It was focusing on the supernatural more than on the natural.

Often, self-limiting beliefs get into your heart when you are focused on facts instead of the truth of the knowledge of God (2 Corinthians 10:5).

Before we look at the three keys of Mark 11:24, let's examine how faith forms the foundation for the Law of Attraction.

FAITH: THE FOUNDATION FOR THE LAW OF ATTRACTION

Hebrews 11:1 is the classic definition of faith: "Faith is the substance of things hoped for, the evidence of things not seen" (NKJV). In this passage there are four keys that show us how to attract the kingdom of heaven by faith. Faith is:

...the *"substance"*—This term means "tangible, substantive, reality, title deed, inventory or substantiate."[12] In other words, faith is real (present). It is a title deed. If I have a title deed to land in Florida, I may never have seen that land, but I can be confident I own existing land. I have the documentation from a credible source.

This term also means "inventory." Inventory is a detailed listing of things in one's present possessions.[13] The Word of God contains 7,700 promises that are our "possessions." This inventory creates an expectation in us. Expectation causes us to have a corresponding action, to "attract" to us what is rightfully ours.

...of *"things"*—This term *things* is the Greek term *pragma*. This word means "things already done."[14] There is an inventory of things that belong to us that are already done.

"hoped"—Obviously, *hoped* means "anticipated or expected" (anxious anticipation, earnest expectation). The Law of Expectation says, "That

which you expect in your heart with conviction becomes self-fulfilling prophecy." Faith is an inventory of things already done, that create expectation in me, which result in a corresponding action.

"evidence"—In a court of law a lawyer produces evidence before the jury. Evidence is data on which a conclusion is based. We all understand about evidence today. Television shows like *C.S.I.* have made us all the more aware of the importance of true evidence. You can say to me, "I haven't been in your living room." Yet, when I examine my living room, I find your fingerprints on my coffee table. Even though I've never seen you in my house, I know you were there based on the evidence. Evidence causes you to believe and even reevaluate what you thought you believed to be true previously. The evidence points to the fact of what God has already done for me.

The author of Hebrews goes on to explain this further in 11:3: "By faith we understand that the universe was formed at God's command, so that what is seen was not made out of what was visible." Now, notice it doesn't say these things were made from things that don't exist, but from things (already done) from the invisible.

Andy Andrews illustrates this from his book *The Traveler's Gift.* In this book the chief character, David Ponder, is an executive at a Fortune 500 company. The company is bought out by another company, and David's job is eliminated. His life begins to spiral downward. At fifty years old, he has difficulty finding a job. Since he can't find work, he eventually loses his house, car, money, and everything materially important to him. The crisis reaches a zenith when his daughter becomes sick and needs an operation that he cannot afford. Realizing he is losing all that is important to him, he contemplates suicide. He tries to call out to God, but in desperation he thinks, *I can't even pray.* He contemplates further options and ponders the fact that he no longer has a purpose. Ultimately, he rationalizes, *Everyone would be better off without me.*

Without further conscious thought, he accelerates toward a tree and his ultimate demise. Gripping his steering wheel and racing toward his doom, he is somehow mysteriously transported back in time. In the past, he meets six or seven different people who expose the real secrets to success in life. He meets President Truman, King Solomon, Christopher Columbus, and others. The last person he meets is the archangel Gabriel. Gabriel gives him a tour of heaven. There he sees rooms filled with money, some with inventions not yet experienced, even some with cures for diseases. There were rooms with photographs of children and stacks of food.

Dazed by what he was seeing and confused by its meaning, he looks at the angel and asks, "Why am I here?"

Finally, the angel answers his question by asking another question, "In despair, why does one person take his life, while another is moved to greatness?"[15]

Reeling in confusion, David responds, "I don't know."

The angel responds, "Circumstances are rulers of the weak…but they are weapons of the wise. Circumstances do not push or pull. They are daily lessons to be studied and gleaned for new knowledge and wisdom."[16]

Struggling to understand the panorama of his sight, he cries out, "What is this place?" Gabriel responds, "This, my friend is the place that never was. This is the place where we keep all the things about to be delivered just as the people stopped working and praying for them. The contents of this place are 'filled with the dreams and goals of the less courageous.'"[17]

This dramatic scene captures the essence of Hebrews 11:3. God has an invisible kingdom filled with the provisions necessary for fulfilling your destiny if you will have faith and courage to receive them.

Here's a real key from this passage. The parent force of the "seen realm" is the "unseen realm."[18] Faith is not "fake it until you can make it." Faith is seeing what is real even though it is unseen. So, when Peter says, "By his wounds you *were* healed," (1 Peter 2:24) it exists in the unseen realm. The problem is that most of us cannot believe until or if we see it manifested in our body. That is why Paul says, "We walk by faith and not by sight" (2 Corinthians 5:7). Faith = Belief + Expectation + Corresponding Action. Faith is the ability to *see what is real,* though it is *unseen.*

I heard my Pastor Billy Joe Daugherty give this example in a recent message in reference to Hebrews 11:3. He said to the affect that, "Presently, there are radio and television waves in this room. We can't see them, but they are there. The reason we know they exist is because when we plug in a television and properly receive its signal, we can get a picture on the screen. The signals were there all the time. We just had to learn to receive what was being transmitted." God's provisions are available to us if we learn to attract them to us (receive what is transmitted).

We don't have to deny the physical realm to recognize the spiritual realm. That is what Metaphysics and Christian Science do. As believers we acknowledge that the physical realm is dominated by the spiritual realm. We don't have to deny cancer exists, but decree that "By His stripes, we are healed." This is why understanding a hardened heart is so important. We must get rid of the unbelief in our lives that causes a hardened heart. Then when what you see in the spiritual world is more real than what you see in the physical world, the spiritual world will dominate your natural world.[19]

This is the point of the story of Elisha and his servant in 2 Kings 6. The king of Syria is at war with Israel. Every time he sets a trap for them, God speaks to Elisha, who warns Israel, and they continually avert the "best laid plans of mice and men." Not understanding the spiritual dynamics of these events, the Syrian king can only assume he is being betrayed by a spy in his camp.

Finally, the king of Syria successfully surrounds the prophet at Dothan. The servant of the prophet arises the next morning to discover the dilemma. In panic he races to the prophet and exclaims, "We're surrounded."

Unmoved, Elisha responds in 2 Kings 6:16, "Don't be afraid…those who are with us are more than those who are with them."

You can almost see the stunned look on his servant's face. Obviously, the product of a higher education math program, the servant sets out to do some addition. As he pokes his head out of the door, he begins counting…50, 100, 200, 300, and 500. He looks back inside and looks at Elisha and counts…1, 2. He must have thought, *I don't know where you got your education, but your math leaves something to be desired.*

Then this unforgettable scene unfolds. Elisha says, "O LORD, open his eyes so he may see. Then the LORD opened the servant's eyes, and he looked and saw the hills full of horses and chariots of fire (angelic hosts) all around Elisha" (2 Kings 6:17).

God's forces then strike the enemy with blindness and ultimately deliver them over to Israel's forces in Samaria. In like manner, the issue for most of us is we only see the physical realm. The chariots of fire didn't just arrive when Elisha's servant's eyes were opened. God's provision existed all the time. The reason we can attract God's kingdom unto ourselves is because God's provision already exists. Calvary's sacrifice set in motion the New Covenant provisions we are to claim as our own.

The key is we need to learn to see with the "eyes of our heart" (Ephesians 1:18). When our soul lines up with our spirit (Hebrews 4:12), we will recognize people, ideas, and resources we've missed up to that time.

APPLYING GOD'S TRUTH IN MY OWN LIFE

This is exactly what I faced in my own life. One day while going for a routine physical exam, my physician decided to run some extra tests. A couple of weeks later I went back for the test results. The doctor said, "Well, I've got some good news and some bad news. Which one do you want first?"

I said, "Start with the bad news and end with the good news."

My doctor responded, "The bad news is you have a potentially terminal disease."

I said, "Well, what's the good news?"

He responded, "It's usually only terminal around 25 percent of the time in your stage."

That's not exactly the good news I was looking for. It shook me for a short while, but I soon came to my senses. I thought to myself, *The physical realm has to submit to the spiritual realm.*

I began to meditate on the truth of God's healing. I began to disassociate myself from the fear of my diagnosis. I also started to confess the truth of God's kingdom about healing. I renewed my thinking to the truth of the knowledge of God. I elected not to take the chemotherapy or steroids (I'm not recommending that process for anyone else). While the results were far from immediate in the natural, about two and a half years later my doctor reexamined me and said, "Your disease burned out and is non-progressive."

I said, "Is that anything like I'm healed?" He nodded his head in affirmation. This lesson, however, taught me something valuable from Mark 11:22-24. It taught me what to do between the "amen" and the "there it is." It taught me what I need to do after prayer and before the manifestation. Mark 11:23 says, "I tell you the truth, if anyone says to this mountain 'Go throw yourself into the sea,' and does not doubt in his heart, but believes what he says,… it will be done for him."

I basically did two things:

Despite all the negative facts of what the doctor had told me, I spoke to my mountain. I confessed the truth of God's Word. I confessed it, I saw myself according to the truth, and I felt the emotions of my healing. I confessed God's Word personal, present tense, and positive over and over every day. It's time to stop telling God about our problem and tell our problem about our God.

I meditated on God's truth until my soul and spirit lined up. I did not "doubt in my heart" (Mark 11:23).

Faith brings the spiritual world into the physical world. Everything you receive and attract from God comes from heaven to earth. We walk by faith and not by sight.

HOW IT ALL WORKS

That brings us full circle back to the three keys of Mark 11:24: ask, believe, and receive:

Ask—I love this term that is used here. *Ask* means "to want or desire something for which you are willing to sacrifice."[20] Asking helps you to bring clarity to your direction and desire. Your mind is a very powerful goal-seeking mechanism. By virtue of being created in God's image, the conscious mind determines truth, and your subconscious mind tells you how to make that truth come to pass. True focus on God-given goals sets your mind to figure out, create, or attract what you are focused on (desire).

Your focus will help you find solutions, guide you to learning experiences, and cause you to recognize opportunities. The problem with most people is that they focus unintentionally or subconsciously. They run their attention on auto-pilot. Their mind is "pre-set" or conditioned by the five aspects of their personal belief system. If their beliefs are erroneous, then in a certain respect, they are "treading water" spiritually. They may not be going backward in their walk, but they certainly aren't moving forward into the abundance God desires for them.

One of the main reasons people don't receive what they want is that they have not determined their God-given goals with clarity. God created you with an "image" that is the "you" of what you were designed to become. Of the five plus billion people on this planet, you are unique. There are no duplicates, and God wants you to flourish and show His image through your distinct personality to His glory.

Often this image gets buried in response to your experiences with parents, friends, teachers, coaches, and other authority figures. You started in God's image with a sense of where you wanted to go in life, and as a child you had no inhibitions holding you back from the expression of that desire. However, somewhere along the line someone said to you:

"You'll never amount to anything."

"This is our 'lot in life.'"

"Don't touch that."

"Don't try this."

"Money doesn't 'grow on trees.'"

After repeatedly having your "hands slapped," many of the desires of your life somehow got lost in the rubble of who you *can't* become. Suddenly, we find ourselves "settling" for less than we are ordained to become. Like Simba in *The Lion King,* we've become less than we are.

"Desire" refocuses us on the "original" truth of our lives. When you consciously and repetitively focus on new truth, your mind generates ways in cooperation with the Holy Spirit to receive it (attract it). Your reticular activating system (RAS— recognition system) begins to notice information, a book, seminars, television shows, or a service you might have otherwise missed.

You may need an answer to the puzzle of a new project to help people grow in their lives. You start recognizing books on the subject. You "run into" people who know information you need. This kind of focus causes your mind to create a new awareness or a "radar," if you will, that brings to your attention solutions and answers that you need. This is not hocus-pocus New Age mentality. It is the Lord ordering the steps of a righteous man. It is a woman who leans not on her own understanding, and her paths are directed by the Lord.

There's a second aspect to the term *desire*. It also means "to long, wish for, want or crave."[21] Psalm 37:4 says, "Delight yourself in the LORD and he will give you the desires of your heart." Most of the time that verse is interpreted as, "Desire God and He'll give you what you want." I do believe our heart is actively engaged in manifesting what we focus on (good or bad). There is another aspect to understanding this verse. If we *delight*—"incline ourselves, desire, favor, desire as valuable"[22]— the Lord, He will give you or put into your heart His desires. One of the ways God leads us is by placing His desires in us. Once we're moved by His desires, it automatically attracts His blessing (cooperation in bringing it to pass). "Desire" is a key in God's direction.

Believe—The term *believe* simply means "take as truth or real." The Law of Belief says, "What I believe in my heart with conviction becomes my reality." We are manifesting in our lives what we truly believe in our hearts. God has given us the measure of faith. It is now up to us to renew our minds to His truth. In Romans 12:2 it says, "We don't conform ourselves to the world's system (the flesh); we transform ourselves to God's laws, by renewing our minds, establishing our hearts, and transforming our personal belief system. Then, we prove, recognize, and manifest the will of God" (author's translation).

That leads us to the Law of Expectation. The Law of Expectation says, "What you expect in your heart with conviction becomes self-fulfilling prophecy." Why? It is because 85 percent of your actions are dictated by your expectation. What you will or will not try is based on your expectations. You get what you expect. Scientists used to believe that people responded to "truth" (information) coming to the mind from the environment. But today, they are learning that our minds respond on the basis of previous experience, and what you expect will happen next.[23]

Neuro-psychologists who study the Theory of Expectancy suggest that we respond as a result of spending our whole lives being conditioned to our environment and our experience.[24] Therefore, our mind is conditioned to what to expect next. Because our mind expects certain things, as a response to this, we often achieve what we expect. That is why it is so important to repetitively hold new positive expectations in your mind, replacing old negative ones.[25] When you begin to believe that God's truth is possible, then your subconscious mind will go to work to make it happen.

The term *expectation* means "to anticipate, to look for as likely to happen, anticipation of good (or bad) in advance, a desire for something, confidence in belief." That is why if you are expecting guests at your home, you clean your house. Your expectation creates a corresponding action. If you are expecting money, you surf the Internet to make a purchase, or perhaps you look for possible places to give. If you are expecting a baby, you start making preparation for the new arrival. You may create a new nursery or buy a crib. If you are expecting a healing, you start making preparations by doing something you could not do before.

If you have ever doubted that you're special, let this quote from Max Lucado encourage you: "You weren't an accident. You weren't mass produced. You aren't an assembly line product. You were deliberately planned, specifically gifted, and lovingly positioned on Earth by a Master Craftsman."[26] God put you on planet Earth, with His image and plan, to bring His plan and your destiny to pass. You must believe in God (His goodness to bless you), and you must believe in yourself.

Expectation doesn't die with age either. Listen to this story Jack Canfield tells of Ty Cobb. When Cobb was seventy years old, a reporter asked him, "What do you think you'd hit if you were playing today?"

Cobb, who was a lifetime .367 hitter, said, "Probably around .290."

The reporter replied, "Is that because of the night games, the travel, the artificial turf, and all the new pitches?"

I can almost see the gleam in Cobb's eye as he responded, "No, it is because I'm seventy years old."[27]

Now, that is what I call "believing" in your self. You can never rise above the level you see of yourself in your heart.

The latest mind research shows that with self-talk and visualization, coupled with training, almost anyone's potential is unlimited. All that means is that the secular community has discovered what has been in the Word of God all along. Confession of the Word (present tense, personal, and positive) and biblical meditation (imagination) change the way you see yourself and God. Once your perspective is changed, you are ready to receive from the kingdom of heaven. One of the jobs of scripture is to change the way you see God and to the way you see yourself.

Receive—This is a Romans 12:2 term, *prove*—to recognize and bring into manifestation what God has done for you. After you've recognized the truth, then you should take action toward your conviction and your highest priority. Once you ask (set your desire) and believe, God will give you a direction and a strategy to bring your dream to pass. Every day do something toward your highest priority. Things don't manifest in your life through the "wish fairy," but by actions or obedience to God's principles.

Then, thank God for His truth belonging to you. Thanksgiving, the attitude of gratitude, puts a guard (a protection) over your heart and mind (Philippians 4:6, 7). Continual thanksgiving will keep you from being distracted by unbelief, and you will be able to receive your desired end.

I remember some years back one of my desires was for God to use me to see people in bondage set free. I spent a season meditating on God's healing power. In the midst of this time, I found myself ministering in a setting outside of West Palm Beach, Florida. It was a multiday meeting, and the last service was on Tuesday. As I was concluding my message, I sensed God point out a woman to me about two-thirds of the way toward the back of the auditorium. I heard Him say, "Do you see that woman?"

I responded affirmatively. He said to me, "She's a heroin and cocaine addict." In some surprise, I responded internally, "Really?" There are some settings you may go into that look like the bar room scene in "Star Wars" and you would expect that. This situation appeared more like a Sunday School class (looked like some really nice people) and it took me off guard.

When the message was completed, I gave an altar call for people to come forward and receive prayer for help. This woman was the last one to come forward. As I moved around the altar praying for people, I finally came to her and said, "What do you want from God?"

She looked at me and replied, "You know!"

I said in reply, "I didn't ask you if I knew. I'm asking you what you want." I wanted her to focus on her desire.

Meekly she replied, "I'm the heroin and cocaine addict you said was here moments earlier. I want you to pray for me."

I looked at her and said, "I won't."

She almost gasped with dismay. "Why, aren't I good enough for you?" she asked.

"No!" I responded. "You're fine. I just know if I pray for you and you don't know Jesus as your Savior, you'll go right back to your habit."

She began weeping, and moments later she received Jesus as her Savior. I said to her, "Now, I want you to see yourself and God differently. It's time for you to be free from your bondage and to experience God's loving abundance."

She looked at me with wide-eyed anticipation. Dramatically, God "ministered freedom" to her for over three hours. I had to leave before she had her final breakthrough.

The following Monday, I received a call from the pastor. He said to me, "Do you remember the heroin and cocaine addict you ministered to on Tuesday? She lives in a drug-infested community over two and a half hours from here. When she went back to her neighborhood, her friends looked at her and said, 'We don't know what you got, but we want some!'"

The pastor told me that about a dozen of her friends showed up at his church that Sunday and gave their lives to Christ. Once her desire was verbalized, she saw herself and God differently. She not only got her touch from God, but it spread to others. Now, that is destiny!

KEYS

We already possess the faith we need to be productive. We need to renew our mind to it.

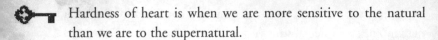 Hardness of heart is when we are more sensitive to the natural than we are to the supernatural.

Faith is the substance (inventory) of things (already done), hope (expectancy) that establishes positive emotion, and corresponding action, based on evidence of what Jesus has already done.

The key to the Law of Attraction is: ask, believe, and receive.

Chapter 8

THE LAW OF CAPACITY
God's Secret to Abundance and Prosperity

MANY LAWS HAVE BEEN PROPAGATED over the years concerning success. One of them is the "80/20 Rule." The "80/20 Rule" says, "Twenty percent of your effort will produce 80 percent of your results. Twenty percent of your people will give 80 percent of your money. Twenty percent of your people will produce 80 percent of your results."

Most of us have heard of the "80/20 Rule." But have you heard of the "16/40/60 Rule." The "16/40/60 Rule" says, "At sixteen you're worried about what everyone thinks about you. At forty you don't care what anyone thinks about you. And at sixty you realize there's nobody thinking about you."[1] That is because they're too busy thinking about themselves. But, I want you to think about you today.

God wants you to operate in abundance and prosperity. Numerous people speak ill about prosperity, as though poverty and lack are more virtuous. I once heard a man say, "I've been rich and I've been poor, and rich is better." The Bible does warn against trusting in riches (Psalm 62:10; 1 Timothy 6:10-17). Indeed, greed and avarice can be distractive and destructive. The real issue is not how much prosperity a person possesses, but the *heart* of the person who possesses it. There is a difference between materialism and wealth. That is why Matthew says, you cannot serve both God and mammon. *Mammon* in its essence is avarice.[2] It is the pursuit of money (materialism). *Prosperity* is "favor, to render successful, increase, advancing in growth or wealth, gain in anything good or desirable, successful progress, profit."[3] Prosperity is the ability to use God's ability to meet any need.[4] It's not wrong to have money; it is wrong when money has you. The following scriptures give valuable insights from God's perspective:

Psalm 35:27b (AMP)—"...Let the LORD be magnified, who takes pleasure in the prosperity of His servant."

Proverbs 8:21—"…bestowing wealth on those who love me (God's wisdom) and making their treasuries full."

Joshua 1:8—"Do not let this Book of the Law depart from your mouth; meditate on it day and night, so that you may be careful to do everything written in it. Then you will be prosperous and successful."

Psalm 1:2-3—"But his delight is in the law of the LORD, and on his law he meditates day and night. He is like a tree planted by streams of water, which yields its fruit in season and whose leaf does not wither. Whatever he does prospers."

2 Corinthians 8:7, 9—"But just as you excel in everything—in faith, in speech, in knowledge, in complete earnestness…see that you also excel in this grace of giving… For you know the grace of our Lord Jesus Christ, that though he was rich, yet for your sakes he became poor (left heaven), so that you through his poverty might become rich."

2 Corinthians 9:6-11—"Remember this: Whoever sows sparingly will also reap sparingly, and whoever sows generously will reap generously. Each man should give what he has decided in his heart to give, not reluctantly or under compulsion, for God loves a cheerful giver. And God is able to make all grace abound to you, so that in all things at all times, having all that you need, you will abound in every good work… Now he who supplies seed to the sower and bread for food will also supply and increase your source of seed and will enlarge the harvest of your righteousness. You will be made rich in every way so that you can be generous on every occasion, and through us your generosity will result in thanksgiving to God."

Philippians 4:19—"And my God will meet all your needs according to his glorious riches in Christ Jesus."

John 10:10—"…I have come that they may have life, and have it to the full."

YOUR CAPACITY TO RECEIVE

These scriptures show that God's intent is not only to supply all of our needs, but grant us abundance and overflow in our lives.

In the past, I have often heard speakers say: "How many of you want to live life out of the overflow?" The obvious idea is that you have more than enough; you have excess. There is abundance. But this is not even the main question. The real question is, "What is your capacity to receive from that abundance?"

One of the major obstacles in many people's lives is that they ask God for things beyond their capacity to receive or maintain. They may say, "Lord, I need a million dollars," but they don't have the capacity to receive it. In fact, 80 percent of lottery winners who have received millions of dollars unwittingly sabotage themselves and end up right back where they were in a few short years.[5] Ninety-five percent of those on diets regain all the weight they've lost. I've also heard it said that 95 percent of people earn within 5 percent of their parent's income when adjusted for inflation. You can only contain what you have the capacity to receive.

The Law of Capacity states, "A person can only receive from God in direct correlation to their capacity to receive from God." God's supply may be limitless, but your capacity may have a "cap."

What is *capacity?* Capacity is the ability "to contain, hold, absorb or receive." It is the maximum holding space. It implies aptitude or mental abilities. Obviously, aptitude means the ability to learn. It is the ability or extent of the mind to receive ideas or knowledge. It further implies the concept to adapt or to recognize. Capacity is the ability "to contain or hold, particularly in the thinking realm."[6] It is the power of receiving ideas or knowledge that brings the possibility of manifestation of those concepts.

Let me give you a simple example from a very large pitcher of water and two cups.

The pitcher, in essence, holds a limitless supply of water. If I have an eight ounce cup and a sixteen ounce cup, I can pour as much water into each cup as it has capacity to hold. After that, it is overflow. My key in receiving from God is not just overflow, but my *capacity* to receive. If I take those same cups and poke a hole in them, then my capacity is further limited to the level of the hole. That hole represents your self-limiting beliefs. The key to receiving more in your life is not simply getting God to send more in your direction, but to also increase your capacity to receive (by eliminating self-limiting beliefs and unbelief) what He is pouring out from His abundance.

One day the former international director on my staff told me a story of a man catching fish. It was a day in which it wasn't just the bugs that were biting. The big fish were biting as well. One fisherman kept reeling in fish that were a foot long, but he kept throwing them back. A nearby fisherman kept watching with an alternating mixture of disgust and amazement. Finally, he couldn't resist the prodding of his curiosity any longer and called out to his fellow fisherman, "Why are you throwing all those big fish back into the lake?" His answer was more disturbing than the fact he didn't keep them. He yelled back, "I've only got an eight-inch pan!"

So often we're just like that fisherman. We ask God in accordance to what *we think* we can do rather than what *He* can do. We come to God with an eight-inch pan and say, "Fill it up," when God's abundance is so much greater. When we consider the size and power of God, sometimes our prayers do not correspond to His ability. Remember Jeremiah's words, "Call unto me and I will show you great and mighty things of which you know not" (Jeremiah 33:3, rephrased).

How, then, do I increase my capacity? Look at the following formula from Matthew 25:14-30:

> [14]"Again, it will be like a man going on a journey, who called his servants and entrusted his property to them. [15]To one he gave five talents of money, to another two talents, and to another one talent, each according to his ability. Then he went on his journey. [16]The man who had received the five talents went at once and put his money to work and gained five more. [17]So also, the one with the two talents gained two more. [18]But the man who had received the one talent went off, dug a hole in the ground and hid his master's money.
>
> [19]After a long time the master of those servants returned and settled accounts with them. [20]The man who had received the five talents brought the other five. 'Master,' he said, 'you entrusted me with five talents. See, I have gained five more.'

²¹His master replied, 'Well done, good and faithful servant! You have been faithful with a few things; I will put you in charge of many things. Come and share your master's happiness.'

²²"The man with the two talents also came. 'Master,' he said, 'you entrusted me with two talents; see, I have gained two more.'

²³"His master replied, 'Well done, good and faithful servant! You have been faithful with a few things; I will put you in charge of many things. Come and share your master's happiness.'

²⁴Then the man who had received the one talent came. 'Master,' he said, "I knew that you are a hard man, harvesting where you have not sown and gathering where you have not scattered seed. ²⁵So I was afraid and went out and hid your talent in the ground. See, here is what belongs to you.'

²⁶His master replied, 'You wicked, lazy servant! So you knew that I harvest where I have not sown and gather where I have not scattered seed? ²⁷Well then, you should have put my money on deposit with the bankers, so that when I returned I would have received it back with interest.'

²⁸"Take the talent from him and give it to the one who has the ten talents. ²⁹For everyone who has will be given more, and he will have an abundance. Whoever does not have, even what he has will be taken from him. ³⁰And throw that worthless servant outside, into the darkness, where there will be weeping and gnashing of teeth.'"

THE LAW OF CAPACITY

Jesus used this parable to teach His disciples the importance of placing value in whatever the Lord gives you. Within these verses in Matthew, the Lord has given us four keys to the "Law of Capacity."

Ability + Resources + Attitude + Stewardship = Capacity[7]

There are *four basic keys to increasing your capacity:*

Ability (v. 15)—the power to do something, skill, power to perform or capacity.[8]

Resources (v. 16)—something to take care of a need, or something to use for advantage…a means to resort to, or supply.[9]

Attitude (v. 16)—a mental conditioning that determines interpretation and response to your environment…. It is the integration of self-image, self-worth, self-esteem, and the ideal self. Attitude does determine altitude, how high you will go with your goals.

Stewardship (vv. 28, 29)—is the concept of management or the dispensing of provision. In other words, it is not only about how much you receive, but how much you keep. There's a major mentality difference between the poor and wealthy. It is not just how much comes in, but keeping the increase.[10] This is why Proverbs 11:16 (KJV) states, "…and strong men retain riches."

#1 KEY
THE PRINCIPLE OF ABILITY

So, if you want to increase your capacity, ask yourself, "What abilities do I need to increase and grow in this area? What resources do I need to appropriate in my area of increase? What kind of mental conditioning do I need to grow in? And how should I learn to manage the increase that comes my way?"

Before we look at some specific applications, let me lay out this concept in the principle which we find again in Matthew 25:14, the Parable of the Talents:

"…it will be like a man going on a journey, who called his servants and entrusted his property to them. To one he gave five talents of money, to another two talents and to another one talent, each according to his ability" (vv. 14, 15).

This passage used to really irritate me. Why would God show favoritism to some by giving them more than others? If you notice, however, he didn't just pass out more talents to his favorites. He gave each one according to their abilities. In fact, the Spanish Bible uses the word *capacidad,* or capacity. Each person received supply according to their capacity to perform. In other words, the more abilities you add to or develop in your life, the greater entrustment from the One who supplies all good gifts (James 1:17).

One of the key ways to increase my capacity is to increase my abilities. A person's abilities would include better understanding of one's giftings, personality, talents, and needed skills. Ability is a God-given skill, talent, or capability to perform a specific task. If you force someone to excel in an area they have no ability in, you unwittingly set them up for failure. You also limit their capacity to receive in that area. We must allow people to discover their unique gifts and then surround them with an atmosphere of encouragement and freedom. The Spirit of God has given gifts to all, so we must help free them from their bondages and self-limiting beliefs.

The "Principle of Ability" works on two levels: (1.) *finding your "genius" level* and, (2.) *finding your productivity level.* I believe everyone has a "genius" level. It is what I call "Finding the Life You Were Born to Live." Your genius level is made up of a combination of *passion + talent + values + destiny = genius.*[11] If you devote your time and energy to discover your passion, talent, and value, you will step into your destiny.

First, look at your *passion.* What is it you love to do? Ask yourself what excites you in life. What do you do when you have free time (hobbies)? What gives you a sense of fulfillment? What strong interests do you have? This reveals your passion or your outreaching affection; the things you will naturally pursue with earnestness.[12]

Then, look at your *talents,* or *skills.* What are you naturally good at? For what kind of things do you get compliments? For what achievements have you been recognized? What have you excelled in, in your past? What do people in your life say are your strengths?

Now look at your *values.* What is really important to you? Ask yourself, "If I could do anything and not fail, what would I do? What do I stand for? Is there something for which I'd risk my life?"

Lastly, consider your *destiny,* or *purpose.* What were you born to do? Where do you seem to make a difference? What are your unique qualities to offer in life?

If you list three or four answers in each category, it will help you discover your genius, or gifting. (Take a moment with pencil and paper and do it right now.) This is where you'll find your highest levels of success—by doing your best at what you do best.

The ability aspect of capacity, however, also has a productivity side. This is where you develop capacities in areas of interest or need. Abilities include not only skills and talents but knowledge. It has often been said, "Knowledge is power." The fact is, however, *applied* knowledge is power. The real fact is: *valuable* knowledge *applied* is power. Many people are filled with knowledge, but it is of no value to anyone. Knowledge used to benefit yourself or others is what creates true value or makes you valuable. Many people spend years acquiring college degrees, but many are filled with knowledge that has no value. To be successful, there's certain knowledge you must appropriate to equip yourself for proper productivity. *Valuable knowledge applied is power.* Your *ability increases your capacity* to achieve your desires.

#2 KEY
THE PRINCIPLE OF RESOURCES

Next, we must examine "The Principle of Resources" to increase your capacity. In the Parable of the Talents, God gives resources according to one's ability (v. 15). Ability will begin to attract people, ideas, and resources according to your most dominant thoughts. Resources are keys to take care of needs. They are something to use for advantage, a means to supply what is necessary. In other words, what do I need to accomplish the task?

Capacity is partially dependent on the assimilation of resources, the materials necessary to succeed. If you want to lose weight, you have to have some expertise beyond "eat less." Once you find a lifestyle that fits you, you need a plan and the resources to carry out that plan. You may have to empty your kitchen cabinets and fill them up with healthier foods. You need a plan to implement your resources properly; a daily or weekly eating schedule for success.

If you want to increase your prosperity, you need to do and accumulate things that increase your *value*. I've heard it said that 90 percent of all fortunes are still made selling familiar products in local markets to regular customers.[13] All you need to start a fortune is a new idea, 10 percent new operating capital, a source of information, a new bent or insight, and the ability to apply it in your "niche" market. Your ability to apply ideas is what separates you from anyone else. You must make your ideas worth something.

I have said for years, "Leaders are readers." The highest paid professionals read on the average of two to three hours per day.[14] Yet 80 percent of American families didn't buy a book last year. I love this quote by Earl Nightengale, "Study any subject one hour per day for five years and you can become an expert on that topic." In other words, it doesn't matter where you are right now, you can put in your hands the resources that make you valuable.

Stop dismissing all the reasons why you *can't* do something, and begin to take actions to put the resources in your hands to advance to the next level. James Allen once said, "A plan consistently, persistently adhered to—good or bad—abundance or scarcity, will produce results in a person's life." If you increase your ideas (good ideas come from a lot of ideas), learn to apply them, consistently, persistently (repetitiously), you will create value; and value creates abundance.

So, read books and magazines, listen to teaching CDs, attend seminars and trade shows. Increase your resources, and in so doing, increase your value. It is important to understand that God will provide all the resources you need to accomplish your dream. Once you renew and focus your mind on God's truth, your subconscious mind, in cooperation with the Holy Spirit, will go to work on generating ideas and actions to accomplish your goals. Next, you'll begin to notice resources you could use to make the dream a reality. You will notice people who could help you that you passed by before. You will suddenly become aware of people, information, seminars, books, or a variety of things you missed up until now. Your internal radar will zone in on everything you need to make your goal come to pass. You'll find yourself motivated to act and to activate your vision. As you begin to imagine how good this will be, persistence will rise up on the inside of you. You will rally all the internal qualities you need to make your dreams come true.

#3 KEY
THE PRINCIPLE OF ATTITUDE

The third part of the formula in the Law of Capacity is *Attitude.* Attitude is a mental conditioning that determines your interpretation and response to your environment. Two people can have the same experience; one person is devastated, the other is motivated. The difference is "attitude." Ephesians 4:23, 24 states, "…to be made new in the attitude of your minds; and to put on the new self, created to be like God in true righteousness and holiness."

The importance of attitude is perhaps best depicted in Jesus' encounter with two of His disciples, James and John in Mark 10:35. Here two of His key disciples try to position themselves for honor and success. "'Teacher,' they asked, 'we want you to do for us whatever we ask.'"

Notice Jesus' reply, "What do you want me to do for you?" It is interesting to me that Jesus didn't rebuke them outright. He simply tried to redirect their misguided hearts.

Their request in verse 37 is for one to sit on Jesus' right hand and the other on His left in His future kingdom. "The rest of the story," as Paul Harvey would say, is that He tries to help them count the cost, while showing them the essence of true greatness.

In the midst of being indignant against the rest of the disciples, Jesus says, "…you know that those who are regarded as rulers of the Gentiles (the world's system) lord it over them, and their high officials exercise authority over them. Not so with you. Instead, whoever wants to become great among you must be your servant, and whoever wants to be first must be the slave of all. For even the Son of Man did not come to be served, but to serve, and to give his life as a ransom for many" (vv. 42-45).

Here is the essence of the attitude of greatness. It is not simply making yourself subservient to others. It is finding your value, your genius, and serving it to other people.[15] True greatness discovers value (abundance always comes out of value) and then finds a way to dispense and serve others with it.

Attitude is a manner of thinking, and then feeling and acting accordingly. One writer, in his study of the five hundred richest people in America, concluded that the one common characteristic they all shared was an attitude of positive expectancy.[16] By acting accordingly, every obstacle or setback becomes an opportunity for benefit.

Attitude is the integration of our self-image, self-worth, self-esteem, ideal self, and a sense of value and significance. Attitude is the manifestation of who you think you are. We live our lives based on who we think we are. It is a reflection also of what you believe about God. You will never rise above the level of what you believe about God and what you believe about yourself in your heart. The problem is we often view God through the portals of our own experience. And quite often that view does not line up with the truth. We try to make God in our image rather than being made in His image. If we change our attitude to view life from God's perspective about ourselves and our world, our life will change dramatically.

Noted Harvard psychologist William James said, "The greatest revolution of my generation is the discovery that by changing the attitudes of your mind, you can change the other aspects of your life." Earl Nightengale suggested, "Attitude is the most important word in the English language." Attitude does determine altitude. In essence, attitude is a mental conditioning of how you see yourself in reference to your environment. How you feel about yourself determines your impact on those around you more than any other factor.

If your attitude is, "I'm unworthy or undeserving of blessing or benefit," you will find a way to make it happen. Why has it been said that the average number of times people try before quitting is less than one. It's *attitude!* Your outer world will always be a reflection of your inner world. If you live in blame, anger, bitterness, self-pity, or irresponsibility, your attitude is one of disempowering self-limitation. How you see yourself (your image) determines what you will or will not try. It determines what you will or will not receive. It determines whether you see yourself as in control or as a victim.

Let me give you an example of an attitude that stands between you and success. It is *courage*. Courage is a mental attitude of facing what is difficult or dangerous (pain) and not withdrawing.[17] Pain is the difference between where you are and where you want to be. Winston Churchill rightly called courage the foremost virtue upon which all others depend.[18]

The simple insertion of a prefix changes the entire meaning of the word. For instance, the prefix "dis" means "separation, negation, reversal, or opposite."[19] When circumstances or environment "dis-courage" us, it separates us from courage, and we tend to withdraw or retreat from trying.

The prefix "en" means "to put into or on, to make or make into." Thus, when we are "en-couraged" by someone in something, we put courage into ourselves and we take the steps to succeed.

Here's an example out of King David's life. First Samuel 22:1-2 states, "David left Gath and escaped to the cave of Adullam. When his brothers and his father's household heard about it, they went down to him there. All those who were in distress or in debt or discontented gathered around him, and he became their leader. About four hundred men were with him."

Now, there's a good way to start an enterprise of any kind. Let's start our business with all our relatives who are distressed, who owe money, and are generally discontented. "Hi! I'd like to introduce you to my new Board of Directors. They've got no money, no success, and they are generally stressed out and discouraged about everything. They're going to share with you how to be encouraged about our endeavors." Right!

Something amazing, however, happens. By the time we get to 2 Samuel 23:8 (NKJV), it says, "These are the names of David's mighty men." What happened to the distressed, in debt, and discontented? Listen to their exploits:

Josheb-Bassahebbeth—…"raised his spear against eight hundred men, whom he killed in one encounter" (v. 8).

Eleazar, son of Dodo, (I always feel better knowing that if the son of "Dodo" can do it, I can do it)—"…stood his ground and struck down the Philistines till his hand grew tired and froze to the sword. The LORD brought about a great victory that day. The troops returned to Eleazar, but only to strip the dead" (vv. 9, 10).

Shammah stood his ground when the enemy banded together in his lentil field. He stood in the middle of his bean patch, struck down the enemy, and won a great victory (vv. 11, 12).

Some of David's men at Adullam heard he wanted a drink from the well at Bethlehem. So three men broke through the enemy line, drew water from the well of Bethlehem, and carried it back to David (vv. 13-16).

What transformed the distressed, in debt, and discontented into men who stood their ground for a bean patch or risked their lives for a cup of water? What inspired a group of malfunctioning individuals into the bravery and temerity to stand against all odds without flinching? It was simply an attitude adjustment. Something they saw in David adjusted their mental conditioning (perspective) to their environment. What was it?

In between these two events were some astonishing moments. First Samuel 30 records one such occurrence. At one moment, David is sleeping in the palace on satin sheets: he was in training to be the next king. Saul, the present king, who was going insane, one day in jealousy hurls a spear at David, causing him to run for his life. The next thing we know,

David is sharing a rock with a coyote. He is surrounded by what most people would call losers. He must feign insanity and live among his enemies. One day while he was out on an expedition, his enemies ransack his city, burn it, and take captive the wives and children of all his men. This is what you call a bad day. About the time you think it can't get any worse, his men become further distraught and decide to take up stones to stone him.

Yet in the midst of these difficult circumstances, an amazing twist takes place in the story. David, greatly distressed by the events of the moment, does something astounding. It says, "...encouraged himself in the LORD" (1 Samuel 30:6, KJV). In the midst of one of the most debilitating times in his life, David looked unto the Lord and drew courage (an attitude that doesn't withdraw out of difficult or discouraging circumstances) into his life to press through the difficult moment to success.

How did David encourage himself in the Lord? The passage doesn't say, but I imagine David rehearsed for himself former successes in his life. He remembered the times when looming failures were converted to successes. He recalled the time when he slew the lion and the bear that threatened his livelihood and even his life. He remembered how he slew a seemingly invincible foe named Goliath.

David's nation, Israel, was embattled against the Philistines, whose army was led by a seemingly unconquerable champion named Goliath. Goliath stood over nine feet tall. He was a combination of Andre the Giant, the Rock, and Shaquille O'Neal. His battle gear weighed almost as much as the young David, who was about to challenge him. Every day Goliath stood at the forefront of his army and taunted his seemingly insipid foe. He intimidated the entire army of Israel. They were all dismayed and terrified. After all, they had a good grasp on height, and no one had the courage to take on this giant.

Like a WWE wrestling event, every day Goliath barked out a verbal barrage targeted to strike fear in their ranks. Saul's army shuddered at the prospect of being humiliated and vanquished. In the midst of this humiliation, David, a young teenage boy, comes on the scene and declares, "Who is this uncircumcised Philistine, that he should defy the armies of the living God?" (1 Samuel 17:26).

This may seem like an odd assertion for David to make, but he was referring to the special relationship that he as an Israelite had before God, which Goliath lacked. For Israel, circumcision was a sign of covenant with God. Covenant, in essence, meant God saying, "If you give me all you have, I'll give you all I have." What David was saying was, "As I stand before this Behemoth, I am keenly aware I have a covenant with God, and this Philistine does not. Therefore, why should I be afraid?" What separated David from everyone else? It was how he saw himself and his relationship with God. He knew that in his own strength he was no match for Goliath, but he had learned long ago to depend upon his God.

For years this young man tended sheep on the backside of the desert ministering to God in worship and meditating on His laws. It was this same young man who wrote, "Blessed is the man who does not walk in the counsel of the wicked or stand in the way of sinners or sit in the seat of mockers. But his delight is in the law (principles that tell you how a thing works best) of the LORD, and on his law he meditates day and night. He is like a tree planted by streams of water, which yields its fruit in season and whose leaf does not wither. Whatever he does prospers" (Psalm 1:1-3).

David sat in the desert for hours imagining himself according to God's truth and not just the facts. It created an attitude in him that only saw the possibility of prosperity and success. Prosperity is really the ability to use God's ability to meet any need. This process had forged in David an irrevocable attitude of invincibility (taking you beyond the possibility of defeat). A person who changes their thinking in this manner only sees darkness as an opportunity, not a probability for the worst case scenario. Successful people not only see more opportunities, they seize them. And seize it David did.

Goliath bellowed out to the ruddy-faced teenage boy with a slingshot in his hands, "Am I a dog that you come at me with sticks? …Come here… and I'll give your flesh to the birds of the air and the beasts of the field!" (1 Samuel 117:43-44).

Undaunted because he had "en-couraged" himself, David replied, "You come against me with sword and spear and javelin, but I come against you in the name of the LORD Almighty, the God of the armies of Israel, whom you have defied" (1 Samuel 17:45).

Why was David able to respond in courage when everyone else had cowered in fear? It is because David had already seen truth ahead of time. It is what I call the "Principle of the Prequel." Prequel is now common nomenclature. The Star Wars movie trilogy was followed by three films of a prequel. A prequel is something that precedes an event. The "Principle of the Prequel" will allow you to see truth before facts ahead of time. It goes beyond being proactive to being "pre-active." This is the key to helping people become "principle" based and not "emotion" based. This is why you tell a child, "It is okay to turn out the lights; there are no monsters in the room. See, look under the bed, and look in the closet. There are no monsters." You tell them what is true. They are not in danger. As true as it might be, they still want the lights on. Why? Fear dominates logic. Emotion dominates truth—until real truth becomes a part of your personal belief system (subconscious).

That is why David wasn't intimidated. He had seen his life in truth ahead of time. Meditation is a way to intentionally increase our faith. David knew how to get ahead ("a head"). David ran toward his "undefeatable" enemy, armed with only a slingshot, smote him in the head, then took hold of Goliath's sword from his scabbard and cut off his head. It was the result of courage that came from being "pre-active."

Courage is not the absence of fear. Think of how many things you would never have done if you had to wait for fear to disappear. You would never have jumped from the high dive, ridden that bike, slept with the lights off, had a date, or gotten your driver's license.[20] Sometimes you "do it afraid," because you know that truth is bigger than facts.

We've got to learn to overcome "psychosclerosis,"[21] the hardening of the attitudes. Nothing is more powerful than a positive mental attitude. Attitude is the perspective by which you view life. Winston Churchill once said, "Courage is rightly considered the foremost attitude upon which all others depend. A positive mental attitude is the key to which expands all the capacity to all the other laws of success. The ability to see truth expands your capacity to receive it."

Now, David had encouraged himself in the Lord. An "en-couraged" man can stand the onslaught of all the doubt around him. David then rallied his men. They pursued his enemy, and they recovered all that the Amalakites had taken (1 Samuel 30:18). Attitude causes you to get all that is coming to you. It increases your capacity.

KEY #4
THE PRINCIPLE OF STEWARDSHIP

The last aspect of the Law of Capacity is *stewardship* (Ability + Resources + Attitude + Stewardship = Capacity). Stewardship is rightly defined as "the management and dispensing of provisions."[22] There is a major difference in the way wealthy people think and the way those who lack think. People who lack think about how much money "I can make." Wealthy people think about how much money "I can keep." A person who has a mentality of lack sometimes will make money, but they will find a way to lose it or spend it until nothing is left. The last aspect of the Law of Capacity not only wants to see increase; it wants to keep increase. Increase can only occur when we position ourselves to receive abundance.

Let me give you an example of what I mean. A recent headline read, "American Airlines Eliminates One Olive from Salads." You might think, "What difference can one olive less on first class salads make toward profitability of the world's largest airline?" Well, in the case of American Airlines, it came out to around $50,000 per year. Sometimes little things can make a big difference.

Now $50,000 may not seem like much money to the profitability of a major airline. However, coupled together with its other cost cutting efforts (stewardship) the results are amazing:

Reducing reserve fuel from 99 minutes to 90 minutes (twice the legal amount) lowered the weight of each flight by 100 pounds. The result was…are you ready for this? …$100 million dollars per year.

Removing kitchens from the cabin class because they no longer serve hot meals in coach, along with adding six new seats in its place will raise income 34 million dollars.

Taxiing to the gate with one engine, instead of two, saves 4 million dollars per year.

It's not simply how much you can make, but how much you can keep.[23]

Abundance takes place when you find a way to invest surplus, not just spend it. It has been said, "A fool and his money are soon separated." Stewardship is a real key in "capacity."

Proverbs 3:1-2 says it this way: "My son (daughter), do not forget my teaching (truth), but keep my commands (truth) in your heart (by meditation into the soul chamber of the subconscious mind), for they will prolong your life many years and bring you prosperity."

What this means is, "Let the meditation (implantation) of God's truth create an image in your heart. Once you see God differently and see yourself according to His truth, God's Word will provide health and prosperity" (parenthetical thoughts added by the author).

Abundance is always the result of value. If you have something of value, people will remunerate you for it. If lots of people share a value, it decreases its worth, because it is accessible from many sources. If few people have your value, it increases its worth. Abundance is always created out of value.

Prosperity is the result of increasing your value in some way. If you create a solution, increase your knowledge, show people a better or faster way, reveal benefit for a clientele, demonstrate a way to access resources, then abundance will follow. Do it faster, improve quality, make things easier, improve service, make a thing less expensive, and people will bless you with increase.

Abundance usually follows doing what you love. When you do what you love, it creates a momentum or an impetus in your heart to pursue a thing to completion. Once I was training people in a seminar, and a woman protested, "Oh, that's great for sales people, but I'm a teacher."

"It's true," I replied. "Public teachers don't make much money, but I can show you a number of people who teach and train who make a lot of money. You must find the right clientele in the right format with the right value."

There are really three aspects of *Stewardship*:

(1) setting your *intention*

(2) *giving and receiving* and

(3) *managing your increase.*

In order to be prosperous, I must believe it is God's will, see myself in line with that truth, and act as if it is true. Every day you must see yourself in accordance to the truth of Scripture.

1. *Intention.* I met one day with a "productivity expert." This man mainly meets with corporations to help them increase sales, customer service, etc. So, I asked him, "What is the main thing you teach to help people become more productive?" He then, gave me this formula: I + M = R. The formula stands for Intention + Mechanism = Results. As I thought about it, I said, "Is that anything like Faith + Corresponding Action = Results?"

He said, "Exactly!"

Then, with a gleam in his eye, he asked this question: "What percentage of the formula do you think is intention, and what percentage do you think is mechanism?"

Wanting to sound intelligent, I thought to myself, "It's 50 percent/50 percent, or 80 percent/20 percent. Then I thought 80 percent/20 percent sounded more intelligent, so I went with the latter.

Smiling broader now, the productivity expert looked at me and said, "No! You're exactly wrong. It's 100 percent intention and 0 percent mechanism."

I immediately protested by arguing how could it be a formula if the second entity doesn't really exist?

This productivity expert explained to me that in their seminars they give people an assignment to show this principle at a lunch break. During the break, the participants are to interact with one another about their main goal (personal or corporate) for the next six months.

After reconvening, the leader of the seminar asks for a volunteer to demonstrate I + M = R. A willing participant is to stand before his peers and yell, with conviction, his goal to the group. Then he is to travel past a "barrier" as a sign of the mechanism.

So, the first participant stands and proclaims, "I want to double my sales in six months." He then proceeds to "walk" past the barrier as a sign of his mechanism to the cheering of his peers, at the prompting of the leader.

The next volunteer cries out, "I want to lose twenty-five pounds in six months." Before they can engage in walking out their mechanism, the leader says, "You've got to do something different than your predecessor for your mechanism."

Somewhat confused, the second volunteer says, "What do you mean?"

The leader responds and says, "They walked past the barrier as a sign of their mechanism. You can do anything but walk."

Momentary confusion disappears as that moment of "revelation" appears in their eyes, and the second volunteer runs past the barrier. Suddenly, it dawns on the group that they are all going to have to come up with an alternative mechanism to everyone in front of them. Mild panic begins to hit the person who is number seventy in line. So, people began to skip, hop, somersault, etc., through seventy mechanisms.

A subtle groan of relief hits the last participant as they squawk like a chicken for their mechanism. Without warning, the leader announces everyone has to go back the other way and do new mechanisms all over again. The mechanisms get more and more innovative (creative) as they reach one hundred forty. Subsequently now, the leader prompts a third try at mechanism displays. Now they have totaled two hundred ten various mechanisms.

At the conclusion, the application is obvious. There are infinite numbers of mechanisms, and if your intention is set, you will find the mechanism to put into action what you truly desire.

How do I bring more increase? Intend it! Find God's will for your life and set your faith in agreement with it, and your subconscious mind along with the Holy Spirit will find a way to bring it to pass (Mark 11:24). Your solution must be believable to you. Intend it (believe it), and it will be yours. One woman told me how God led her to raise money for a new truck for their Christian school's football coach. She met obstacle after obstacle and was ready to quit. Suddenly, she remembered I + M = R (F + CA = R). She went to the car dealer and put down a down payment of $1,000. She said, "If I don't have the remaining money in thirty days, you can keep my $1,000. All of a sudden new strategies came to her. What she hadn't been able to do in several months was completed in fifteen days.

Negative feelings block ideas from coming to you. Faith in God's provision opens the windows of heaven.

2. *Giving and Receiving.* The Scripture says, "Give, and it will be given to you. A good measure, pressed down, shaken together and running over (overflow), will be poured into your lap. For with the measure (capacity) you use, it will be measured to you" (Luke 6:38). Galatians 6:7 says, "…for whatever a man sows, that he will also reap (NKJV)." Second Corinthians 9:6 states, "He who sows sparingly will also reap sparingly, and he who sows bountifully will also reap bountifully."

Giving is a powerful action that brings increase into your life. It is a kingdom law that you have to see in your heart. When you are giving you are saying, "I possess excess."[24] It is why the wealthiest people on the planet are the greatest philanthropists.[25]

If you focus on getting out of debt, it will cause you to create dominant thoughts of debt. What you focus on you tend to create. When you focus on lack and scarcity and what you don't have (and you fuss about it with family and friends), this is what you tend to create. You attract it because you are looking for it. If you are looking at what you can't afford, you'll perpetuate it.[26] Charles Filmore said, "The spiritual substance from which comes all visible wealth is never depleted. It is right with you all the time and responds to your faith…and your demands on it."

The real reason giving works can be seen in the four laws of Genesis 1:26 (chapter 1). It is the initiation and authorization of man on earth to attract God's provision from the kingdom of heaven. It is a kingdom law that, once you believe and act on it, moves the hand of God. For some of us it is a huge paradigm shift to think that giving is increase for us, not depletion. Proverbs 11:24 says, "One man gives freely, yet gains even more; another withholds unduly, but comes to poverty." In the natural, it doesn't make sense, but in God's system kingdom law brings increase.

3. *Managing Your Increase, or Stewardship.* For years multiple books have given simplistic keys for wealth:

Tithe (Pay God 10 percent.)

This process or principle allows God to protect your funds or storehouse (Malachi 3:6-12).

Save 10 percent (Pay yourself 10 percent.)

Invest 10 percent.

Live off of 70 percent and don't spend more than this.

This may seem obvious, but not when you consider over 70 percent of people live from paycheck to paycheck. Only 56 percent are saving for retirement at all.[27] One financial expert suggests 90 percent of your problems can be fixed with good financial mangement. Spend less and invest more and abundance will follow.

People have a tendency to spend emotionally. Two-thirds of Americans have a minimum credit card debt of $5,000 or more.[28]

If you were to save $25.00 per week at *10 percent* interest, the result would be:

5 Years	10 Years	20 Years	30 Years	40 Years
$7,808.	$20,655.	$76,570.	$227,933.	$637,628.

at *12%* interest:

$8,249.	$23,234.	$99,915.	$352,999.	$1,188,242.

Similarly, if you were to save $3,000 per year at age 15 at 10 percent for 5 years, your total investment of $15,000 with compounding interest would be $1,600,363.40 by age 65.[29]

The Law of Capacity is a real key to abundance. Abilities acquired + resources assimilated + positive attitudes achieved + stewardship that promotes proper management and investment = increased capacity.

This is a formula that creates a systematic approach to a guaranteed increase. This is how you overcome the kind of self-sabotaging actions that limit how much you can receive. It's time to *take the limits off.*

If you're not living up to your full potential, it is likely life is affording you more than you have the ability to receive. All of life is the result of a proper belief system aligned with proper principles.

The Law of Attraction is not simply about your finances, however. It spills over into every area of your life. Let's look at the Law of Attraction and you.

KEYS

Prosperity Exercise

 Meditate on prosperity scriptures (see the *Barrier Busters Manual* list at the end of chapter 4 if you need help finding scriptures).

See it for yourself. Imagine what it will look like (including how you can bless others).

Ask yourself what is the next step you need to take.

Set your intention and watch for your mechanism.

Do your "Genius test" (pp. 181 & 182). You always do best at what you do best.

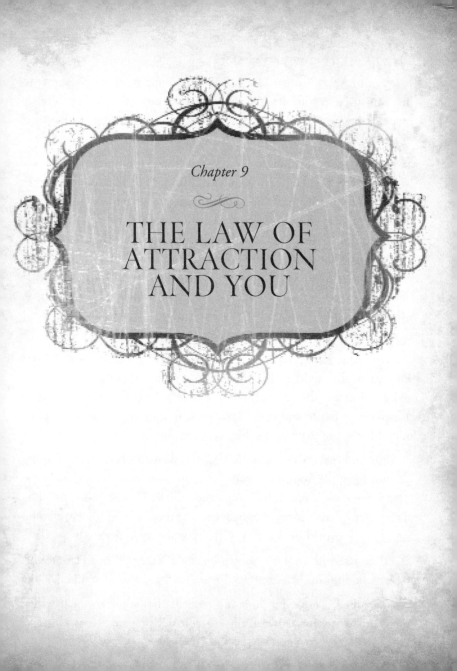

Chapter 9

THE LAW OF ATTRACTION AND YOU

THE LAW OF ATTRACTION is the law where all other laws gather. It is the "prove" of Romans 12:2. It is your ability to use God's ability to meet any need in your life. You can attract the provision God has already prepared for you by renewed thinking and a transformed personal belief system (faith).

As I was meditating on this one day, the thought came to me, "This is like a race." In Hebrews 12:1-3 it says it this way, "Therefore, since we are surrounded by such a great cloud of witnesses, let us throw off everything that hinders and the sin (weights) that so easily entangles, (besets, KJV) and let us run with perseverance the race marked out for us. Let us fix our eyes on Jesus, the author and perfecter of our faith, who for the joy set before him endured the cross, scorning its shame, and sat down at the right hand of the throne of God. Consider him who endured such opposition from sinful men, so that you will not grow weary and lose heart." In this passage the author compares life to a race.

Some time back I was in San Antonio holding a series of meetings. This particular night at Family Praise Center, I thought of a way to vividly illustrate the idea of a race before several thousand people. I turned to the pastor and said, "I want you to find the best athlete in this house. I'm going to challenge him to a race."

Unbeknownst to me, a professional basketball player from Europe was sitting on the front row. I called him up front, not yet knowing what he did. So, I asked him if he was a good athlete. He responded humbly, "Pretty good." The crowd laughed, because most of them knew who he was. Then I learned he was almost thirty years my junior.

I then asked Justin if he thought he could "take me" in a race around the large auditorium. He smirked, "Yeah," as the crowd roared in delight.

Unabashed, I looked at him and replied, "I'm going to totally decimate you!" Now the crowd really roared. As I prepared to race him, I said, "There is only one stipulation. Neither of us can leave the starting line until I say, 'Ready…set…go!' If either of us breaks the stipulation, we will be disqualified."

As we poised for the start of the race, I bellowed out, "Ready…set…go!" Justin broke out of the blocks, leaving me in the dust. I yelled out, "Hold it, hold it, hold it."

As he came back to where I was standing somewhat confused, I said, "Please notice in this passage it says to run the race without any hindrances. I need a hindrance."

I asked one of the church associates to jump up on Justin's back. Then I looked at my game competitor and again asked, "Do you still think you can 'take' me?"

Still overly confident, he confidently confessed, "Yes!" After taking off his suit coat, revealing his six-pack abs rippling through his dress tee-shirt, and taking off his dress shoes, he still insisted he could win.

So I started out a second time. "Ready…set…go!"

As he charged out a second time, he once again heard my protest, "Hold it, hold it, hold it!" I pointed out that the passage also says to run without weights. So I got two large muscle laden youths to act as weights and to hold his feet. Rather cockily I asked, "Do you think you can beat me now?"

Weighted down on his back and legs, he let out a disgruntled, "No!"

Without hesitation I barked out a third time, "Ready…set…go!" As Justin labored to move at all, I ran circles around him, taunting as I went, all to the great delight of the crowd.

This is how some of us are trying to live our lives. Jesus said He came to give us abundant life. He wants us to live a life without limitations. All we have to do is get around the track to the finish line, and it is all ours. Instead, we labor through life talking about how hard it is, because we're weighted down.

In this passage in Hebrews 12, the term *hindrances* refers to "a non-sinful set of besetting circumstances, attitudes, or actions that hold you back." This hindrance includes things like worry, fear, discouragement, anger, bad relationships, ignorance, double-mindedness, or the biggest one of all, self-limiting beliefs. (Some of these concepts could be construed by some as sins.)

The weights in this illustration refer to sins. There is really only one sin. Unbelief. Everything else is a manifestation of unbelief, including things like lust, pornography, drugs, alcohol, adultery, homosexuality, hate, etc. We are trying to live according to a limitless Gospel, but the weights keep us in a limited expression.

The biggest problem for most people is the inability to change. They seem to experience the same problems for a lifetime, accentuating a wrong identity and falling back into old patterns. As believers, they don't seem to be able to get what's "in them" "out of them" to manifestation.

How many times have you seen somebody legitimately seem to repent, and then they end up right back where they started shortly thereafter? People get converted, but they can't get past their unforgiveness. They want to go to the next level, but the fear of failure holds them back. They have new ideas and dreams for their life, but they lack the peace to step out and try them. They desire a good marriage, but they seem to lack the ability to adapt. They have a vision but lack the faith to implement it. They hate who they are but lack the self-control to go in another direction. They remain stuck in their depression, poverty, pornography, being overweight, drugs, alcohol, or worst of all—mediocrity. Mediocrity is the worst, because it is like false advertising. We shouldn't belong to the King of the universe and remain mediocre. (We are made for success and to dominate our environment.)

Our self-limiting beliefs (sometimes manifesting in the flesh of the world's system) keep us from our true destiny and our true provision. The Law of Attraction is the doorway to your eternal destiny. The Law of Attraction is attracting people, ideas, and resources to your life automatically. You are attracting your most dominant thoughts; it is an automatic law. You reap what you sow (Galatians 6:7) and receive what you believe (Mark 11:24).

Before we look at this principle in a broader focus, let me ask you a question: what is the greatest compliment you've ever received? Maybe someone complimented you on your appearance. Perhaps someone recognized an accomplishment you had. Maybe someone told you how great your kids are.

Recently, I was at an alumni event at my alma mater. I ran into several local parents who were raving about my middle son, Daniel, who is a youth director in Tulsa. They were going on and on about how "D-Mac" had impacted their kids' lives or turned "so & so's" life around. It was really a gratifying experience as a parent.

However, let me tell you of one of the greatest compliments I've ever received. After a speaking engagement, my host was taking me to the airport the next morning. He had miscalculated the time to the airport, and we were arriving much too early. To compensate for the early arrival, he suggested we stop at a café for breakfast. When we sat down to order, I started telling stories, and we started laughing and having a good time. Pretty soon, our fun started spilling over to other tables. The other customers were getting in on our fun. By the time our waitress came to take our breakfast order, she looked at me and said, "I don't know what you're drinking, but I want some."

The frivolity continued, and when she came back to let us know our order would be up soon, she said, "Seriously, I don't know what you're on, but I want it."

Finally, when she came back to our table with our order, she said more seriously, "I don't know what you have, but I want it."

I had her sit down, and I shared the joy of a life fulfilled by truly knowing Jesus. She rededicated her life to Christ right there and turned a confused life around. To tell you the truth, I can't think of a greater compliment than, "I don't know what you have, but I want it."

Yet, for many Christians, there is so little distinctiveness in their lives than that of an unbeliever. Their self-limiting beliefs have masked the limitless Gospel in their lives. Genesis 26:12-13 tells the remarkable story of Isaac. Beginning in verse 12, it tells how Isaac dealt with a famine, "Isaac planted crops in that land and the same year reaped a hundred fold, because the LORD blessed him. The man became rich, and his wealth continued to grow until he became very wealthy. He had so many flocks and herds and servants that the Philistines envied him."

Sadly, Christians are not envied by the world. When we ask, "Do you want what I've got?" their response might be, "No, I've got enough problems of my own, and at least I don't have to obey all those rules."

Religion has robbed many of the vitality of a living God who wants to bless them with all His riches in Christ Jesus (Philippians 4:19). I'm not just talking about material well-being, but to experience all the love, joy, peace, faith, solid relationships, and a happy marriage that God ordains for our lives. All of this is masked in the discovery of the Law of Attraction. You receive what you believe. You manifest your dominant thoughts.

Most of us attract by default. We just think we don't have any control over it. Our thoughts and feelings are on auto-pilot, so most things are brought to us or manifested by default.

Look at Galatians 6:7-8: "Do not be deceived: God cannot be mocked. A man reaps what he sows. The one who sows to please the sinful nature (flesh), from that nature will reap destruction; the one who sows to please the Spirit, from the Spirit will reap eternal life (the God kind of life)." Anyone who thinks he is not practicing this verse is deceived. It is an absolute law, whether you believe it or not. You are either sowing to the Spirit or sowing to the flesh, and you will reap after its kind. The term *reap* means "to collect, gather, gain, obtain, get a return, seize, or in essence attract."[1] *Attract* means "to draw to, to cause to move towards, unite with, incline to engage."[2] In other words, whatever you sow you draw toward yourself. If you sow to the world's system, that is what you will attract. If you sow thoughts of scarcity, that is what you are reaping. If you sow thoughts and actions of abundance and productivity, you will reap and attract abundance.

This is one of the spiritual laws of God that controls our lives. It does not have to be believed to work. Those who fail to believe this law still reap its consequences anyway. It is like the "Law of Gravity." If you jump off the roof, you will hit the ground; and likely you will hurt thyself. The Law of Attraction is an immutable law that is at work in our lives. You are reaping from the dominant thoughts that have been sowed into your life.

Early in my ministry, I had a need to be needed. I found myself surrounded by need everywhere I went. I was working seven days a week, twelve hours a day. I couldn't understand how every week turned into a ninety-hour week. I could never meet all the needs. After one year of ministry, at twenty-five years old, I admitted myself into a hospital exhausted, with debilitating headaches. I was literally rendered dysfunctional.

In desperation I called out to God to heal me. I was mad at God and I cried out, half in desperation and half in anger, "Lord, I'm doing all this stuff for You. Now heal me!"

As soon as I said it, I heard God speak to me as clear as a bell. "You're not doing all this for Me. You're doing this for you."

I was devastated, but it was true. Because I had a need to be needed, I was attracting people's needs to myself. I repented (changed my thinking), and the moment I did, I was instantly healed. I put my clothes on, and I was released from the hospital. I went back to my church and canceled every program. I had not only exhausted myself, I had exhausted everyone else in the church. I promised my congregation that I would never add another program unless God directed us. I began to point people to Jesus as their source. Amazingly, in six months our church quintupled.

The psychologist Carl Jung said it this way, "What you resist persists." *The Secret* suggests that the anti-war movement creates more war. The anti-drug movement creates more drugs, because you are focusing on what you don't want.[3] Jack Canfield quotes Mother Theresa as saying, "I will never attend an anti-war rally. If you have a peace rally, invite me."[4] Remember, you attract whatever your dominant thoughts are.

I have an acquaintance in ministry who tells a story of how the Law of Attraction changed a man's life. He said that he did a business meeting in Dallas, with about one hundred businessmen in attendance. When he returned the following year, one of the men who had attended the seminar the year before gave this account. He said, "Last year when you were here, you shared a concept that revolutionized my life. I'm a businessman who makes deals with other companies. Until last year, I negotiated deals based on what it could do for me and my company. You told us not to make deals based on what I can get, but who I can bless. That mentality just helped me to close a five billion dollar deal."

Why? Several things come to mind. First, he disassociated himself from the world's system. Secondly, he renewed his mind to God's system of blessing others. Thirdly, his renewed mind and established heart found ways to bless others and find solutions for their needs. It resulted in a transformation of his life and a solution for the other company. Ultimately, it manifested blessing for himself and blessing for the company he helped. Blessing always attracts blessing. Like Abraham, God blesses us to be a blessing (Genesis 2:3). The act of blessing is a kingdom law that attracts the kingdom's provision.

Look at the heartbeat of Scripture. Romans 12:14 says, "Bless those who persecute you; bless and do not curse." Why does the Bible say that? Is it because bad people curse and good people bless? No, it is because thinking and operating in God's system attracts the provision of the kingdom of heaven.

Luke 6:27-31 says it this way, "But I tell you who hear me: Love your enemies, do good to those who hate you, bless those who curse you, pray for those who mistreat you...do to others as you would have them do to you. (The "Golden Rule" still rules, v. 31). Truly life and death are in the power of the tongue (Proverbs 18:21). Cursing others is like the old adage, "It's like drinking poison and expecting someone else to die."

The passage continues, "If you love those who love you, what credit is that to you? Even sinners love those who love them... But love your enemies, do good to them, and lend to them without expecting anything back. Then your reward will be great..." (v. 32-35). This is "good success" (Joshua 1:8). So many people destroy themselves by attracting the very thing they curse or its attitude, when God wants them to possess the blessing only love can afford them, because it frees their spirit.

In Romans 3:20 Paul says, "Therefore no one will be declared righteous in his sight by observing the law; rather, through the law we become conscious of sin." We need to acknowledge and repent of sin, but God knows the key to productivity is not sin consciousness, but righteousness consciousness. When you truly understand who you are in Christ and what He's done for you on the cross, you will not try to acquire things through the flesh.

All sin is the result of lack. Once you sense lack, if you don't trust God, you will try to meet your need in the flesh (doing God's will in your own ability). Once you realize you are in right standing with the God of the universe, not based on what you've done, but receiving what Jesus has done for you by faith (righteousness—Romans 3:20-26; Romans 10:3,4; Philippians 3:7-9), it alleviates the need to try to get something from the world's system (anyone or thing other than God). In fact, Matthew 6:33 (NKJV) says, "Seek first the kingdom of God (God's system to receive His provision and resources from the kingdom of heaven), and all these things (the context is your daily needs) shall be added to you."

This is why all great teachers of confession, affirmation, or self-talk all agree in the power of the words "I am." Your confession should be personal (I am), present tense, and positive. Your personal affirmation imprints an image in your heart. Remember, principles don't change a person, images do. Your declaration (confession), done repetitively, will create an image in your heart. Your heart will then move you to manifest God's provision in that area.

If you declare, "I can't afford this," "I am always late," "I am feeling old," "I am always tired," etc., you are sending a signal to your heart to follow after the image it is creating.

Instead, confess, "I am excited about having God's abundance." "Let the weak say, I am strong" (Joel 3:10, KJV). "Lord, I am thrilled I am full of Your strength."

Similarly, this is why James says, "…pray for each other so that you may be healed" (James 5:16b). It is why James earlier stated, "…God resists the proud, but gives grace (ability) to the humble (submitted to the view and opinion of God). Therefore, submit to God. Resist the devil and he will flee from you…purify your hearts, you double-minded…humble yourselves in the sight of the Lord, and He will lift you up" (James 4:6-10, NKJV). Whatever system you're operating in, you will attract to yourself. Praying for others' healing attracts the kingdom's provision for you. Humility attracts God; flesh manifested in pride (doing things your own way without God) tells God you'll handle this on your own.

I have a friend who has attended my Bible Study for about three years. He is a very successful sales person in his company. One day he was very excited over a deal he made. It was a very large deal, and the customer agreed to the stipulation of the sale. A series of events caused the customer to unethically "stiff" my friend on the deal. The ensuing conversation became heated over the customer's impropriety. After a few days, my friend came to himself and the understanding of the Law of Attraction. He called the customer back, and here's how the conversation unfolded. He told his client, "I don't approve of what you did, but I forgive you." The client thanked him, and they parted company peaceably. Within twenty-four hours a new client contacted him with a deal twice as big (around $1.5 million).

THE LAW OF CONTROL

This is the Law of Control in action. The Law of Control says, "A person is positive in life to the dimension they are in control of their lives." Most people feel out of control of their lives. Acting in the flesh subjugates a person to the world's system. Most people, then, give in to their circumstances, and life dictates to them, instead of them dictating to life.

How many times have you heard statements like these?

"I've started a new diet…for the sixth time."

"I've finally learned an effective time management system…if I could only find it."

"My business has finally grown this year, but my teenage son is rebellious and into drugs."

"I'm busy, busy, busy…busy! But at the end of the day I wonder what I've done."

"I'm sick and tired of being sick and tired."

"I really seemed to change for the better last month at the seminar, but now I don't see any perceptible change."

"I want to stop having these thoughts, but I just don't seem to have any will-power."

"I started a new exercise program…again."

"My marriage is flat, I know I love my mate, but I just can't continue. Counseling doesn't seem to help."

In years of helping people toward productivity, I have found that most people (unwittingly) feel that life is dictating to them rather than they are dictating to life.

Self-control is the ability to do what I truly want to do in the context of God's will, when He wants it done. (It is the ability to control my environment by the Holy Spirit.) It is the basis God uses to help us overcome mediocrity and consistent failure. Self-control is ability and power to overcome stagnation, being immobilized, fear of failure, and repeated shortcomings. It is indeed the power to overcome self-determinism and the trapped feeling of "it's always going to be this way." When Jesus stood up in John 14:30 and declared, "…the prince of this world…has no hold on me...", He was saying, "It's God who is in control, and as long as I'm submitted to Him, I'm in charge of my own destiny...not satan, not the government, not humanists, not terrorists, not activists, not circumstances, not bosses, not temptation, not loss and devastation. I have the God-given ability not to be dictated to, but to dictate. When you understand this law, it means you are unstoppable!

At this moment, America is suffering from a huge lingering feeling of fatalism. The lingering effects of Iraq, Afghanistan, Enron, mistrust of government officials (all the way back to Watergate), scandal, avarice, manipulation, and greed have left an indelible imprint of pessimism. Intellectuals have become so open-minded their brains have fallen out. The party spirit has left tragedy in Aruba and in the life of Anna Nicole Smith. There's a lingering feeling that nothing great will happen, so there is an undercurrent resolve to go for short-term pleasure. There's some concocting feeling of impending doom.

The real question becomes, how does anyone really control their lives, let alone the environment around them? Is anyone really in control of their lives?

The answer is found in Genesis 1:26: "Then God said, 'Let us make man in Our image, after Our likeness; let them have dominion...over all the earth....'" Man was to have dominion, or to dominate his environment; mankind was to be in control of their destiny. Men and women were to dictate to life, not have life dictate to them. Notice it clearly says, "...*let them* have dominion." They were to clearly dominate the environment in which they lived. Man was in charge of earth (Psalm 115:16).

Let's review the four key principles or laws that proceed from Genesis 1:26:

God gave legal authority to dominate the earth to mankind.

God did not include Himself in this authority structure on earth.

Interference or intervention from the supernatural realm must be authorized by man.

God subjugated Himself to His own laws.[5]

This is similarly reflected in the Lord's Prayer. "This then is how you should pray: 'Our Father who art in heaven, hallowed be your name, your kingdom come, your will be done on earth as it is in heaven.'"

God's kingdom comes to earth by man's invitation, authorization, and initiation. God limited His rule, domination, and control of earth to man's authorization of His kingdom. That is why salvation is not universal. Salvation is subjugated to a man or woman's invitation. God's control of your environment comes from your operating in obedience to His kingdom laws.

THE YOKE'S ON YOU

Matthew 11:28-30 tells us how we can best initiate this process; "Come to me, all you who are weary and burdened, and I will give you rest (or grace, see Hebrews 4:1, 3, 10). Take my yoke upon you and learn from me, for I am gentle and humble in heart, and you will find rest for your souls. For my yoke is easy and my burden is light."

In essence, Jesus is telling us what the key to the control of our lives and experience is. When we are burdened and things are out of control, we are encouraged to cast our care on Him and authorize or access His grace (God's ability to do what our ability cannot do).[6] Then, He says four basic things to do:

"Take my yoke upon you"—This phrase was used to describe oxen being yoked together in Hebraic culture. Two oxen were yoked together to distribute the load. Often a small ox would be yoked to a large ox,

and wherever the large ox would go, the small ox would follow. Direction and shared load made the task simpler. Jesus is simply saying that we feel loaded down and burdened because we've attempted to face the hardships of life on our own. We are to submit ourselves to His yoke and let Him carry the load.

Abide—This is the principle Jesus tried to share later in John 15:7. "If you abide in Me, and My words abide in you, you will ask what you desire, and it shall be done for you (NKJV)." The word *abide* means "to await submissively, to fix ones attention upon, unbroken fellowship, to continue, stand, to be uninterrupted."[7] It connotes consistency. If we learn to wait on Jesus submissively (submitting to truth), if we fix our attention on Him and not be distracted from truth by circumstances or facts (this comes through meditation), if we continue to stand (effectively or invincibly, Ephesians 6:14, in Greek) steadfast in opposition, in uninterrupted communion with God, He says, whatever we ask will be manifested (done for us). This becomes a prerequisite to the Law of Attraction.

Thus, if the enemy can't destroy you, then his main tactic is to distract you. I'll never forget going to a doctor for a routine visit a few years back. During the examination, the doctor asked me to come back for a series of tests. These were the kind of tests where they run a tube up your nose and down your throat into your lungs. When the report on the biopsy finally came back, he said it indicated a potentially terminal disease in my lungs. It's easy to understand how news like this can be devastating, and it was. After the initial shock, I did what David did and strengthened myself in the Lord by remembering all He had done for me up to this point. I reminded myself that God is my healer despite the fact that I was experiencing the effects of a serious health issue.

The dilemma I faced was that my beliefs and my reality didn't match. When beliefs and experience don't match, that is one of the greatest spiritual opportunities for a believer. It becomes the crossroad that determines your destiny. This is what "abide" and "yoke" really mean. Fact and truth are not always the same thing. The fact is, I have a potentially terminal disease, but the truth is "I am healed by the stripes of Jesus." It is the challenge between the "amen" and the "there it is."

Now is the time to wait submissively, to fix your attention on truth, to have unbroken fellowship, to continue, to stand, and to maintain uninterrupted communion with Him. Everything in life will challenge this process. Circumstances, fear, worry, people's comments, and their past experiences are often contrary to your desired results. Do not be surprised if everything yells at the top of its lungs information contrary to your hopes. The burden and weight will begin to mount. Where your focus is during this time will determine your mental state. If you focus on contrary evidence, that will decide your expectations. If you focus on truth and open the gateways to your heart by transforming your personal belief system, your expectations will rise to meet your dreams. By the way, the journey will be better as well.

For me, the journey took over two years. During that time Ephesians 3:16-20 came alive to me: "I pray that out of his glorious riches, he may strengthen you…through his Spirit in your inner being, so that Christ may dwell in your hearts through faith…." Christ dwells in your spirit by salvation, but He dwells in our hearts by faith.

"…and I pray that you, being rooted and established in love, may have power, together with all (God's people) the saints, to grasp how wide and long and high and deep is the love of Christ…."

Once love is "rooted" in you, every little circumstance contrary to hope doesn't send you in a downspin. You don't think things like, "I'm not perfect, so God wants to punish me." I'm rooted in His love, and God has thoughts of love, mercy, and grace toward me (Hebrews 4:16).

"Now to him who is able to do immeasurably more than all we ask or imagine, according to his power that is at work within us" (Ephesians 3:20) is an amazing verse. When that verse got in me, the burden lifted, and so did the boundaries that kept me from experiencing God's abundance. There's an empowering within me that won't be denied that is rooted in Christ's unfathomable love.

Eventually, a couple of years later, while getting an insurance examination, the doctor came back with the report: Sarcoidoisis burned out and nonprogressive. I've never had a problem since. "Yoked" with Jesus is good.

"Learn of me" is the next point of solidifying the Law of Control. God has laws that govern His kingdom. Laws are principles that tell you how a thing works best. Remember, the kingdom of heaven is the location and resources of God. The kingdom of God is the governance, rule, territory, or the system by which the kingdom of heaven is accessed.[8] God's rule comes into your environment, and it becomes His territory as you submit to kingdom law in your heart and act accordingly. "Learn of me" is an invitation to that system.

The next principle in Matthew 11:28-30 is "…for I am gentle and *humble in heart…*" This word *humble* means "to submit to the view and opinion of (God)."[9] In other words, my soul submits to the spirit, and the two chambers of my heart submit to the view and opinion of God. When your heart is submitted to God's laws, the dynamics of the kingdom are activated and begin to work in your life.

Here are the results: I find rest for my soul (my soul and spirit are aligned), my yoke is easy, and my burden is light. How do I know if something gets in my heart? First, it becomes easy for me, and second, it will change the image of how I see myself. Once a revelation is truly in your heart, truth becomes easy, and it changes how you see yourself and your environment. You are in control.

Noted psychologist Martin Seligman wrote a book called *Learned Optimism*. In his writings he suggests that 80 percent of people feel helpless to change their circumstances.[10] This is similar to Steven Scott's percentages of drifters (25 percent), pursuers (25 percent), achievers (24.99 percent) and super-achievers (.01 percent) (see page 30). Around 75 to 80 percent of people feel helpless to change or control their environment. The term *stronghold* in 2 Corinthians 10:5 confirms this. This term means "feeling powerless to change something, though it is contrary to the Word of God."

This principle is depicted in Paul's trial in Acts 24. Paul is on trial before Felix, the Governor of Caesarea, for inciting a riot with the Gospel. During the trial, Felix's wife Drusilla, a Jewess, asks her husband to hear Paul's faith. So Paul speaks to them on righteousness, self-control, and judgment (Acts 24:24).

When I read this, I was stunned. Paul gets an opportunity to share about his faith, and he chooses righteousness, judgment, and self-control. Righteousness and judgment I understand. After all, everyone needs to understand righteousness. Righteousness is right standing before the Father, not based on what you've done, but what Jesus has done. You receive it by faith (Romans 3:20-22; Romans 4:3-13; Romans 5:1; Romans 10:3, 4; Philippians 37-9). It is our basis of qualification (Colossians 1:12) and confidence to receive from God.

I also understand his sharing about judgment. After all, everyone will someday stand before the judgment seat of Christ. Unbelievers will be judged to eternal punishment. A separate judgment for believers, not having to do with eternal destiny, will take place for the works they have done (2 Corinthians 5:10). So, sharing about judgment makes sense to me.

The question becomes, of the three things he does share, Why does he choose to share on self-control? The term used here in the KJV is *temperate*. This term to most people means "moderation in indulgence of appetite, or passions."[11] It appears that Paul is saying to Felix, "It might be a good idea to lighten up on the cheesecake." Is Paul trying to get the Governor to cut back on the "carbs"? Is his Christian witness simply suggesting that Felix cut back on "Big Macs" in his diet or to curb the Playboy Channel from his viewing habits?

This, however, is a mischaracterization of this word. The term *control* (self-control) used here is not so much restraint as "mastery or to have power over."[12] In other words, Paul looked at his judge and said, "I know I'm on trial, and you're my judge, but be advised. God's in control here, and so I'm not going to die before my time." The Bible says, "Felix was afraid and said, 'That's enough for now.'"

One thing about the Law of Control is that it often appears that you are not in control. Sometimes it looks worse before it gets better. Sometimes it is "darkest before the dawn." Perspective makes a huge difference in your ability to recognize what God is doing. Perspective helps a person to see the relevancy of the moment in lieu of the whole picture. Paul was thrown into prison so many times he probably had a "frequent stayers" card. I can imagine the devil thinking when it happened that he had won. The conversation with his demonic henchmen probably went something like this: "Well, we've finally got him bottled up. By the way, what's he doing in there?"

The henchmen respond, "Nothing! He is just writing."

Paul was "just writing" over 50 percent of the New Testament. The Law of Control will allow you to see what God is doing, often in trying circumstances. This law simply means operating in spiritual authority. Spiritual authority is the recognition and operation in delegated power. God has authorized you to dominate your environment. During rush-hour traffic, police officers only have to raise their hand to stop traffic. They don't use their own strength to accomplish the task, but the authority invested in them by the local government. The government and system of heaven have authorized you to function on His behalf in all of your circumstances.

God made us to dominate our environment when operating in kingdom law. This is His kingdom and His will be done on earth as it is in heaven (Matthew 6:10). This earth, however, has been given to man (Psalm 115:16). This is the dominion that is spoken of in Genesis 1:26. And, this is the reference to the "keys to the kingdom" that bind the works of the enemy and loose God's kingdom in your life. This is the key that brings the Law of Attraction to your life.

Some years back, I was doing some work with a man whom I admired greatly as a hero in the "faith." Some things began to disintegrate in our relationship. We had some disagreements on how things should work. This man decided at Christmastime to terminate our working relationship.

That meant that by January 1 (about two weeks), I needed to establish my own separate itinerary. You don't just "launch" a new itinerary in two weeks. Most places book months in advance for their special speakers. This was also one of the driest times in my life. I hadn't felt God's presence or heard Him speak to me in months. As you can imagine, this set of circumstances brought a certain amount of upheaval to my household. Our financial security was also being severely challenged during that time.

In the midst of this crisis, I found myself sitting in a church service in my home church in Tulsa, Victory Christian Center. During the service, I felt the presence of God come on my life for the first time in months. In that moment, I heard God speak to me. He said, "I want you to give (a large sum of money) in the offering tonight."

My first thought was, "Oh, great! I haven't heard from You in months, and the first time I hear from You, You want money." I simply blew it off.

A matter of moments later, I heard the same word. "I want you to give (a large sum of money), in the offering tonight." I struggled with what I was hearing—my financial security was being challenged, and God wants my money—what's up with that? I wanted to respond, "Satan, I rebuke you in Jesus' Name."

A few moments later, I heard the exact same urging. I knew it was God, and I told my wife God's instruction. Judy is somewhat security motivated and was hesitant to take action.

I looked at her and I said, "I know this is God!" With some degree of fear and trepidation, Judy wrote the check.

I can't begin to tell you what happened next. Within about a week my phone began to ring off the hook. I got calls from people saying things like, "I know that this is short notice, but could you be here in two weeks?"

I was thinking, "Well, let me check my calendar. Yeah, I guess I'm available any of the fifty-two weeks." My calendar filled with speaking engagements. It was the greatest year in the history of my ministry, both in results and finances.

What happened in this circumstance? My obedience (operation in the kingdom law of giving) authorized and initiated the kingdom of heaven's provision. The Law of Attraction, under the Holy Spirit, brought me people, ideas, and resources according to my growing dominant thoughts. It allowed me to stay in control of my environment. God brought productivity out of seeming devastation.

It is time for abundance! It is time for living a life without limits!

It is time for the Law of Attraction to attract to yourself people, ideas, and resources to your most dominating thoughts. Now it's time to believe.

KEYS

Are there weights or hindrances you need to rid yourself of to step into your destiny? Identify self-limiting beliefs. Replace them with new empowering beliefs.

The Law of Sowing and Reaping is automatic. It is important to target your sowing. Target what you need and sow a seed.

Move in the Law of Control by targeting your heart.

John 15:7 says to abide in Christ and abide in His Word." Ask yourself daily, "Am I waiting submissively on God? Am I surrendering to His view and opinion?" Sometimes I ask people, "Is God smarter than you?" People usually laugh at this remark, because the answer is obvious. Then, I usually follow this question with the statement, "Then why don't you act like it?"

What area are you learning from Him right now? What self-limiting belief are you targeting with the antidote of truth?

A submitted (yielded to the view and opinion of God) heart is what makes life easy. You'll know if something is in your heart because it is easy for you, and if it has changed how you see yourself. Consistency is the key. Don't give up your meditation and confession before it "kicks in" and changes your heart.

Chapter 10

I BELIEVE, I BELIEVE, I BELIEVE

THROUGHOUT THIS BOOK we have endeavored to study the laws that God has established in His kingdom so that every believer can live a fulfilled life as He originally intended it since creation. To summarize, here are six laws to success and the process of faith:

The Law of Control—People are positive in life to the dimension they are in control of their lives.

This is the foundational law. This is the law that says, "I'm in control of my destiny. I have dominion over my environment. By obeying kingdom law I initiate and authorize God's kingdom provision in my life.

The Law of Capacity—I can receive from God in direct correlation to my *capacity* to receive from God.

This is the defining law. This is the law that defines the dimension that I receive from God, as I increase my capacity by the following formula: *Ability + Resources + Attitude + Stewardship = Capacity.* Increased capacity increases my ability to receive from God's limitlessness. When my endlessness meets God's limitlessness, nothing is impossible.

The Law of Belief—What I believe in my heart with conviction is my reality.

This is the *"catalyst law."* It is the law that ignites all other laws. Faith (belief) is the law. Romans 3:27 calls it the *Law of Faith.*

Notice that Paul calls faith a law. Faith is governed by law, as are electricity and gravity. Electricity has been in the earth since creation. We saw its evidences, but it was through a bald-headed guy with a kite and key (Benjamin Franklin) that we came to understand there were laws that governed its use. Similarly, we know that faith exists, but we must harness the laws that govern its use. Once an individual understands this process, we can use faith to tap into the provision of the kingdom of heaven.

The Law of Expectation—That which I expect in my heart with confidence becomes self-fulfilling prophecy. Eighty-five percent of our actions are the result of our expectations. In other words, what I choose to do or not do are the result of what I expect to happen in my heart.

This is the *Law of Mobility*. I initiate action as the result of expectation that faith brings me.

The Law of Attraction—I attract to myself people, ideas, and resources according to my most dominant thoughts. My renewed thinking, established heart, and transformed personal belief system attract the kingdom of heaven to myself.

It is the *Law of Manifestation*. It is an automatic law. You are attracting to yourself your dominant thoughts. Like attracts like. The system you are in (the world vs. heaven) is the system you attract. What you sow is what you are reaping. You are attracting what you sow.

The Law of Correspondence—Your outside world corresponds directly to your inward world. What you believe inwardly in your heart is what you *are* manifesting. Your renewed thinking is the key to what you attract.

This is the *Automatic Law*. It is automatically working in your life. Your inward world is busy constructing your outward world. Your subconscious mind is busy making what your conscious mind says is true come to pass. Your subconscious mind is searching for solutions to your "truth."

The catalyst to this process is the *Law of Belief*.

RESET THE IMAGE IN YOUR HEART

In the classic animated hit movie *Shrek,* the film concludes with its characters doing a rendition of the 1970s singing group The Monkeys' "I'm a Believer." Led by Donkey who "hip hops" and "bee bops" across the screen, it concludes with the repetition, "I believe, I believe, I believe, I believe…." He is joined by the Three Blind Mice bumping into one another echoing, "I believe, I believe, I believe, I believe…." Soon all the fairy-tale characters are similarly reverberating, "I believe."

It's a very funny and cute scene, but unfortunately that's the way a lot of us think we learn to believe. If I can just say I believe often enough, some pixie dust will fall from the heavens, and it will be so. That's the wonderful world of positive thinking, and it's valuable. Unfortunately, it's not all the answer. The problem is we give all the promise and half the answer, and that creates frustration in people. Frustration often leads to lethargy, and ultimately people quit trying. That's why you hear people say things like, "I tried that faith stuff." "I used to pray all the time." "That prosperity stuff only works for the people on the platform." (Or, at least we think it.)

So is there a more complete answer? The Law of Belief states, "What a person believes in their heart with conviction becomes their reality."

Unwittingly, that is true of every person. You are manifesting what you believe. You may or may not be aware of what you truly believe, but basically that is what "issues" (Proverbs 4:23) are coming to pass in your life. The combination of your: (1) social environment, (2) authority figures, (3) self-image, (4) repetitious information, and (5) experience has created a belief system in you, and you are living them out. The real question becomes, "How do I get my beliefs to line up with what is my true destiny? How do I convince myself to do the things that cause higher levels of success in my life? How do I obtain new levels of the manifestation of faith? How do I create beliefs that manifest the highest levels of productivity in me?"

What is "faith"? Faith simply defined means "persuasion, conviction, trust, or reliance." Faith is belief plus expectation plus corresponding actions. (Belief, expectation, and corresponding action = faith.) The word literally means "to trust in, rely on, or adhere to."[1]

So often, people are confused by the seeming enigma of faith. How much faith do I have to have to get stuff to work? How much faith is enough faith? Faith doesn't get God to do something; it recognizes what He has already done. Faith doesn't believe God "will," but God "has." You already have enough faith (Romans 12:3; Galatians 2:20; 1 Peter 1:2; Matthew 17:17-21; Luke 8:50). Once you remove the areas of unbelief in your life, you'll begin to adhere to God's laws.

Faith is like an illustration I often use. I call a volunteer forward and ask them to face the audience, while I stand behind them and give them instructions. The instructions go something like this: "Put your arms out to the side. When I tell you to, fall straight backwards." It usually solicits a howl from the crowd and looks of hesitation from the participant. The next set of instructions sound something like this: "If I like you and I'm a man of integrity, I will catch you before you hit the ground. If not, you're going to have a nasty little fall." Some participants will readily fall back expecting to be caught. Some, wondering what the point of the illustration is, glance back to make sure they don't need to break their fall. As the "catcher," I try not to catch them too early to test their trust level. This is a picture of belief. Are you willing to implicitly trust the principles of faith and fall blindly into their source of fulfillment? For most of us our trust is based on our past experiences, past social environment, how we're feeling about ourselves, past advice from respected authorities, or some other self-limiting belief. To sum it up honestly, we're not always immediately adhering to new truth.

So how do we increase our trust so we can rely on truth until we adhere to it? This word *adhere* means "to stick like glue." It gives you a sustaining quality that produces success.

The only way to increase the manifestations of your beliefs is to increase the image you have of yourself in your heart. Just as we shared earlier about writing on the tablets of your heart, in order to change your personal belief system, you must target the subconscious mind in the soul section of your heart. In other words, you've got to break your set points, self-limiting beliefs, or comfort zones and realign them to God's truth.

It's like the difference between a thermostat and a thermometer. A thermometer simply measures temperature. A thermostat sets the temperature. For instance, if I come into a room and I think it is too hot, I may adjust the thermostat. If it is 78° and I think I want it cooler, I may set it at 75°. Within moments the meter of the air conditioner kicks in and runs as it goes to 77°. It continues running at 76° and 75°. At 75° it stops, because that is where the thermostat is set. If you still think it is too hot, you can reset the thermostat to, let's say, 72°. Again, the air conditioner runs until it falls to 72° where it is set.

It's the same thing in our own lives. If we want to change how we believe, we've got to reset the thermostat of our hearts. We have to break self-limiting beliefs, set points, or comfort zones to go to new levels.

It's interesting to hear Robert Allen make this quote: "Everything you want is just outside your comfort zone." Everything you want for your progress is just beyond where it is comfortable to go after it.

How, then, do you break comfort zones and increase the manifestation of your faith? Once you go through the questionnaire of the five areas of your personal belief system, quantify your comfort zone with a tag. For instance, my bad relationship created a fear of rejection. Or perhaps, my parents' constant harping about money caused a feeling of lack. My rejection caused me to feel unloved. Maybe my drugs are an excuse not to try because I feel a need to be punished. Discouraging circumstances made me feel like a failure, and I've lost my joy.

Once you've identified the root, establish its antidote (see the *Barrier Busters Manual* or a fairly complete list at rmmimpact.com). Using the above example it might look like this:

Comfort Zone (Self-Limiting Belief)	Antidote
1. Fear	1. Love/Righteousness
2. Lack	2. Prosperity
3. Fear of Rejection	3. Love
4. Discouragement	4. Joy
5. Resentment	5. Forgiveness

Then, assemble scriptures. Through the meditation process, see yourself according to the truth. Then establish confessions as affirmations. Affirmations are statements as though they are a completed act. Remember, your confessions must follow the 3 P's: personal, present tense, and positive.

Let me amplify on this process:

Personal

Start with the two most powerful words in the English language, "I am." The soul, in the subconscious mind (SCM), takes all "I am" statements as a command, a directive, or authorization to make it come to pass.

Solidify this process through repetition. (Remember, it takes twenty-one days to create a new habit.)

Remember God's name is "I am" (Exodus 3:14; John 8:58).

Make your confessions about yourself, not for others.

"I am watching Jonathan clean his room." (wrong)

Versus

"I am effectively communicating to Jonathan about neatness."

Include an "-ing" action word.

Add a verb for the power of evoking "new images."

"I am a good speaker." (wrong)

Versus

"I am loving the effective messages I am speaking."

Present Tense

Describe what you want as though you already have it. This is called "faith."

"I am celebrating the fact that I am the righteousness of God."

Positive

Always state your confession in the positive.

The SCM does not hear the term "no."

That means if the SCM hears "I do not have fear," it evokes images of fear.

"I am no longer afraid of flying."

Versus

"I am enjoying the thrill of flying."

Keep it brief.

Make it specific. Vague confessions produce vague results.

"I am believing for increase."

Versus

"I am enjoying making (a certain amount of money) per month."

Add words of emotion.

Add feeling words.

"I am maintaining at 177 pounds."

Versus

"I am feeling fit at 177 pounds."

This process sets in motion the transformation of your personal belief system. You eliminate self-limiting beliefs and reinforce faith according to truth.

I want to take a moment to tell you how this principle relates to the amazing miracle healing of Dodie Osteen. Dodie is the wife of the late John Osteen, and the mother of current Lakewood Church Pastor, Joel Osteen, and four other children. In 1981 Dodie was diagnosed with metastatic liver cancer. It has been my privilege to be casually connected to Dodie and more intimately with other members of the family.

In October of 1981, Dodie had a series of tests run at the City of Faith Hospital in Tulsa, Oklahoma. The tests included a grueling schedule of CT scans, upper and lower GI, bone marrow biopsy, and uterine biopsy.

Then came the haunting words, "Your cancer is malignant." As you can well imagine, the emotions ran from astonishment to denial. Then came the seemingly final pronouncement: even with chemotherapy she only had a few weeks to live.

In the midst of the ensuing struggle, Dodie realized it was not the faith of her "famous" friends that would deliver her. It wasn't the faith of Oral Roberts, Kenneth Hagin, or her husband, John, that would "turn the tide." It would be her own belief that would set her free. Transforming her own personal belief system was the key to her healing.

She began her fight by refusing to lie in bed or letting others take care of her. She was committed not to act sick.[2] In fact, she set the Law of Attraction into action grabbing a hold of James 5:16, "Pray for one another that you may be healed," and Luke 6:38, "Give and it will be given to you."

Dodie began to extend herself to others, and her reaction was, "When I forced myself to pray for someone else, my health came back to me."[3]

She began to establish in her heart that God could not lie. If His Word said it, then it was true. The process, however, was a war. She said she never wavered in her heart, but she did in her head. According to Hebrews 4:12, her soul and spirit sometimes warred. There were times to deal with fear and times to cast down imaginations (2 Corinthians 10:5). She laughed at symptoms but warred against thoughts. She disassociated herself from thoughts of the worst case scenario with new empowering thoughts of God's Word. The greatest struggles came in the lonely moments during the middle of the night.

During this time her family treated her as if she were normal. It kept the "pity parties" minimized and helped her focus on God's truth. She meditated on forty scriptures every day before beginning her day. She made herself congruent with heaven's will. The truth permeated her mind and heart. Confession was a daily ritual, as well as a struggle. She watched over the words of her mouth. She confessed, *"I am* healed." She began to see it in her heart. Finally, in November 1983, the Osteen's personal physician, Dr. Reginald Cherry, told the family they could never really appreciate the magnitude of the healing of metastatic liver cancer in Dodie's life.[4]

What happened in this miracle moment? Dodie enacted the tenets, the laws of Romans 12:2. She wasn't conformed to the world's system. She was transformed by the renewing of her mind and establishment of her heart. Suddenly, she "proved" the good, acceptable, and perfect will of God. Dodie identified her boundary (sickness). She then identified her antidote, healing. Pursuing its end, she meditated on the truth repetitively until it imprinted an image on her heart. Her rethinking attracted God's already existing provision from the kingdom of heaven. What an incredible story of God's provision and a person's belief, the Law of Attraction working in both of their desires.

Let me tell you the story of a woman in one of my seminars. Often people come to me with desperate, debilitating situations. She looked haggard and exhausted. She hadn't slept through the night in ten years. She looked at life through the lens of the pain of Fibromyalgia. At seventy-two years old, life was something to be endured, not something to look forward to each day because of the constant pain.

She took two biblical meditation CDs from my Barrier Busters Series, one on peace and the other on healing. The CDs took her through the five steps of biblical meditation. As she got "still," she positioned herself to receive new truth. As she listened to the "peace" CD, within two weeks she was sleeping through the night.

She then listened to the CDs on "healing." Repetitively day and night she heard the truth on healing. She then began to see herself according to the truth. She not only saw herself well, but well enough to reach out and help her peers. She began to strategize her future by taking Bible school classes. She was increasing her capacity. She started confessing the truth: "I am excited about feeling whole as I minister to my peers."

She began to thank God for her healing. Like Judge Lee's healing in chapter 3, she saw the pain eradicated and destiny secured. She attracted to herself the kingdom of heaven and its provision.

HOW'S THAT WORKIN' FOR YA'?

Recently, in a setting where I was speaking, I talked with a woman who was having a number of problems in her life. She was struggling with her weight, struggling with relationships, and just struggling to have any sense of victory in her life. I would make some suggestions about renewing her mind and God's kingdom laws, and it was always met with this phrase, "I believe that, but…" over and over again.

In the midst of her telling me what she believed, suddenly the spirit of Dr. Phil came on me, and I interrupted with, "How's that workin' for ya'?"

Inquisitively, she looked at me, and then it hit her. She was more interested in defending what she believed than changing to a life of productivity and fulfillment. "You see, I'm not interested in winning the debate," I told her. "I'm interested in helping you."

The impact of what I'd said hit her, and she began to weep. What she was doing wasn't working for her. Somehow in this country, everything has been reduced to the bottom line of winning. Politics is all about winning. It has stopped being about new ideas to help people and has taken on the identity of winning at the cost of impugning anyone not like you. In certain corridors of the church, we defend the truth we've always been taught (the defense of truth is important), and we attempt to crucify new phraseologies and methods that attempt to help people. Sometimes we break tradition, and it upsets our comfort zones. The participants in the first move of God are calling people back to "what they had," while God is getting ready to do a new thing (at least for us). People defend where they are even if it is mired in mediocrity, or worse, defeat. We huddle in our sanctuaries of truth, without realizing we reflect more of the world's system than God's. Our divorce patterns are the same as the world's. Our lifestyle patterns reflect everyone else's. We're caught at the same place in our life year after year, yet we are caught defending what we've always been taught.

That's when I looked at this woman and said, "What if I told you there was a 'secret' that could change your life? What if I told you there were truths in God's Word that have been overlooked in our generation, but once we grasp them it will change everything in your life? Would you be interested?" She responded with tears and laughter. Her life has been on a new course ever since. She's had some setbacks, she sometimes struggles with identity, but in the midst of three steps forward and two steps back, she is finding herself moving one step forward. And, for the first time in years, she is both fulfilled and productive.

I'll never forget helping one of my former staff members through this process. She was a beautiful and intelligent young woman. She was bright and very capable. Tragedy out of her past left her feeling unloved and abandoned. She always felt she never measured up to God's standards. She felt unacceptable. She viewed herself as inferior, and in her eyes she believed God was mad at her.

After some hours of counseling with her, I showed her how to do biblical meditation on love and righteousness. (Not understanding "righteousness" is often a symptom of people feeling that God is angry with them.) Over a period of about a month, I started seeing a tremendous change in her. No longer was she up one day and down the next. She didn't feel "in" one time and "out" later. Her confidence started to soar. She was more relaxed. I noticed she wasn't trying to be accepted by performance, but she was performing at a higher level. When she left our ministry, she left whole, fulfilled, and feeling loved. Today she has her own business and is thriving.

Perhaps this book is best summed up in the experience of Jesus in the synagogue in Nazareth (Luke 4:18). Jesus walked into a service one day and unrolled the Scriptures to Isaiah 61, where it says, "The Spirit of the Sovereign LORD is on me, because the LORD has anointed me to preach good news to the poor. He has sent me to bind up the brokenhearted, to proclaim freedom for the captives and release from darkness for the prisoners, to proclaim the year of the LORD's favor."

Few passages are richer in their pronouncement of freedom and productivity. I want you to zero in on this one phrase, "recovery of sight for the blind." Every time I hear someone amplify on this verse, they say this refers to the spiritually blind or the physically blind.

Indeed that is true, but there is something more here. This same phrase is used in Mark 6. Here Jesus is about to feed the 5,000 (20,000 if you count women and children) with 5 loaves of bread and 2 fish, and it says, "and *looking up to heaven,* he gave thanks and broke the loaves" (emphasis mine). You know the story, the loaves and fish were multiplied, and they fed the crowd until they were satisfied and 12 basketfuls were left over.

Here is the amazing revelation. The phrase "looking up to *heaven,*" is the same phrase Jesus used in Luke 4 for "recovery of sight."[5] In other words, Jesus realized the impossibility of His task and He had to "recover sight." He had to regain or maintain His identity in the kingdom (2 Corinthians 5:17 for us). Once you see God for who He is, and understand your new identity in Him, once your mind is renewed to His truth, you will not only obey kingdom law, you will attract the kingdom of heaven to your life. You will attract people, ideas, and resources according to your most dominant thoughts. Jesus attracted heaven's miraculous provision, and a multitude of people were fed by one boy's snack.

God has made you to live a life without limits! It's time to discover who you really are and experience abundance! It's time for productivity theology! It's time for you to step into your destiny! *Remember, you are unstoppable!*

KEYS

Remember, the Law of Belief is more than just positive thinking.

Reset set-points by:

Identifying your set-point.

Establishing your antidote.

Making a confession list.

Employing new empowering beliefs.

EPILOGUE:

The "Law of Attraction" must never be relegated to the temporal realm alone, but must be given an eternal perspective. It is a law of productivity, but not only in the temporal. It is the initiation into eternity. God does bless us here on earth, but the "greatest secret" is salvation by grace through faith in Jesus Christ. Everything pales in comparison to the peace that is provided in salvation in Christ. If you've never made that decision, and it is in your heart to do so, repeat the following prayer:

"Jesus, I receive You into my life as my Savior and Lord. I say yes to Your ways and Your system. I submit myself to You. From this day forward, I will live for You. All that I say, do, and will be are Yours. You are my Savior and my Lord. In Jesus' name, Amen."

If you've prayed that prayer, please contact our ministry (rmmimpact.com) or contact a local pastor who can encourage your growth as a Christian.

ENDNOTES

INTRODUCTION

1 Barna website, www.barna.org

2 James Strong, *The New Strong's Exhaustive Concordance of the Bible,* The Greek Dictionary of the New Testament (Nashville: Thomas Nelson Publishers, 1990), p.42.

Greek Dictionary of the New Testament, p. 42.

Joseph H. Thayer, *Greek-English Lexicon of the New Testament* (Baker Book House, Grand Rapids, MI), 1977, p.352.

Noah Webster, *New World Dictionary of the American Language* (Cleveland and New York, 1957), p. 296, p. 1548.

3 Ibid., p. 462.

CHAPTER 1

1 Rhonda Byrne, *The Secret* (Hillsboro, OR: Atria Books, Beyond Words, 2006), p. 6.

2 James Strong, *The New Strong's Exhaustive Concordance of the Bible,* The Greek Dictionary of the New Testament (Nashville: Thomas Nelson Publishers, 1984), Entry #932.

3 Dr. William McDonald. Dr. McDonald is a language professor at Oral Roberts University. These insights were gleaned in a conversation with him. The kingdom of God equates to the supernatural element of God. God's rule is primarily in the heart of man. God's rule on earth is activating God's supernatural provision by yielding to it in our hearts.

4 Byrne, p. 4.

5 Ibid.

6 Byrne, *The Secret* DVD.

7 Ibid.

8 Brian Tracy, *Change Your Thinking, Change Your Life* (Hoboken, New Jersey: John Wiley and Sons, Inc., 2003), p. 84.

9 James Strong, *The New Strong's Exhaustive Concordance of the Bible, Hebrew Chaldee Dictionary Section*, Entry #6754; *Webster's New World Dictionary, College Edition* (The World Publishing Company, USA, 1957), p. 978.

10 Ibid., *Strong's Hebrew Chaldee Dictionary*, Entry #1923; *Webster's*, p. 849.

11 Myles Munroe, *Understanding the Power of Prayer* (New Kensington, PA: Whitaker House, PA, 2002), p. 14.

12 Myles Munroe, *Rediscovering the Kingdom* (Shippensburg, PA: Destiny Image Publishers, Inc., 2004), p. 28.

Chapter 2

1 Brian Tracy, *Maximum Achievement* (New York: Simon & Schuster, 1993), p. 4.

2 Ibid., p. 45.

3 Ibid., p. 48.

4 Ibid., p. 53.

5 Brian Tracy, *Getting Rich Your Own Way* (Hoboken, NJ: John Wiley & Sons, Inc., 2004), p. 23.

6 Stephen Scott, *Mentored by a Millionaire* (Hoboken, NJ: John Wiley & Sons, Inc., 2004), p. 3.

7 John 10:10.

8 James Strong, *The New Strong's Exhaustive Concordance, Greek Dictionary of the New Testament*, (Nashville: Thomas Nelson Publishers, 1990), Entry #4053, p. 57.

9 Brian Tracy, *Create Your Own Future* (Hoboken, NJ: John Wiley & Sons, Inc., 2002), p. 241.

10 Rhonda Byrne, *The Secret* (Hillsboro, OR: Atria Books, Beyond Words Publishing, 2006), p. 9.

11 Ibid., p. 9.

241

12 Ibid., pp. 10, 12.

13 Ibid., pp. 12-13.

14 Noah Webster, *American Dictionary of the English Language*, 1st ed. (San Francisco: Foundation for American Christian Education, 2002), p. 43.

15 *Webster's New World Dictionary, College Edition* (The World Publishing Company, USA, 1957), p. 568.

16 Joseph H. Thayer, *Thayer's Greek-English Lexicon of the New Testament,* (Grand Rapids, MI: Baker Book House, 1977), p. 357.

17 James Strong, *The New Strong's Exhaustive Concordance of the Bible, Greek Dictionary of the New Testament* (Nashville: Thomas Nelson Publishers, 1984), Entry #165, p. 9.

18 Dr. Jim Richards, *Grace: the Power to Change* (New Kensington, PA: Whitaker House, 1993), p. 36.

19 James Strong, *The New Strong's Exhaustive Concordance of the Bible, Greek Dictionary of the New Testament* (Nashville: Thomas Nelson Publishers, 1984), Entry #3339 & 3340, p. 47.

20 Dr. William McDonald. Dr. McDonald is a language professor at Oral Roberts University. These insights were confirmed in a conversation with him. The kingdom of heaven equates to the supernatural element of God. God's rule is primarily in the heart of man. The kingdom's rule on earth is activating God's supernatural provision by yielding to it in our hearts.

21 Webster, *New World Dictionary*, p. 1546.

22 Webster, p. 244, *American Dictionary*, p. 35.

23 Webster, *American Dictionary*, p. 97; Webster, *New World Dictionary*, p. 1546; Strong's, *Greek Dictionary of the New Testament*, Entry #3339, p. 47; Thayer, p. 405.

24 Strong's, *Greek Dictionary of the New Testament*, Entry #342, p. 11; Webster, *American Dictionary*, p. 58; Webster, *New World Dictionary*, p. 1770.

25 Brian Tracy, *Maximum Achievement* (New York: Simon & Schuster, 1993), p. 17.

26 Strong's, *Exhaustive Concordance of the Bible, Hebrew and Chaldee Dictionary*, Entry #8176, p. 119.

27 Ibid., Entry #8444, p. 123; Webster, *American Dictionary*, p. 124.

28 R. C. H. Lenski, *The Epistle to Hebrews and the Epistle of James* (Minneapolis: Augsburg Publishing House, 1966), p. 141.

29 Kenneth S. Wuest, *Wuest's Word Studies from the Greek New Testament*, vol. 2 (Grand Rapids, MI: Wm. B. Eerdmans Publishing Company, 1973), p. 20.

30 Lenski, p, 145. Lenski says of Hebrews 4:12, in place of soul and spirit the writer of Hebrews now uses heart for the center of our being.

31 I. V. Hilliard, *Mental Toughness for Success* (Houston, TX: Light Publications, 2003), p. 47.

32 Strong's, *Greek Dictionary of the New Testament*, Entry #1771, p. 24; Thayer, *Greek-English Lexicon*, p. 29.

33 pepweb.org

34 Strong's, *Greek Dictionary of the New Testament*, Entry #1381, p. 24; Webster, *New World Dictionary*, p. 1172.

35 Mark Victor Hanson, *The One Minute Millionaire* (New York: Harmony Books, 2002), pp. 76-77.

36 Ibid., p. 74.

37 Ibid.

38 Byrne, *The Secret* DVD, quote from Dennis Waitley.

CHAPTER 3

1 Jim Richards, *Breaking the Cycle* (Huntsville, AL: Impact Ministries, 2002), pp. 16-18.

2 Message shared by Jerry Savelle.

3 James Strong, *The New Strong's Exhaustive Concordance of the Bible, Greek Dictionary of the New Testament* (Nashville: Thomas Nelson Publishers, 1984), Entry # 4053, p. 57.

4 Ibid., Entry # 5228, p. 74.

[5] pepweb.org/Anthony Robbins, *Awaken the Giant Within* (New York: Free Press, 2003), p. 66.

[6] R. C. H. Lenski, *Interpretation of the Epistle to Hebrews and the Epistle of James* (Minneapolis: Augsburg Publishing House, 1986), p. 532.

[7] Brian Tracy, *Change Your Thinking, Change Your Life* (Hoboken, NJ: John Wiley & Sons, Inc., 2003), p. 187.

[8] Lou Tice tape series.

[9] Ibid.

[10] Strong's, *Greek Dictionary,* Entry #4982, p. 70.

[11] *Webster's New World Dictionary, College Edition* (The World Publishing Company, USA, 1957), p. 302.

[12] Conversation with Mike Stephens.

[13] Myles Munroe, *Understanding Potential* (Shippensburg, PA: Destiny Image Publishers, 1991), p. 145.

CHAPTER 4

[1] Don Colbert, *Deadly Emotions* (Nashville: Thomas Nelson, 2003), p. 6.

[2] Rhonda Byrne, *The Secret* (Hillsboro, OR: Atria Books, Beyond Words Publishing, 2006), p. 29.

[3] I. V. Hilliard, *Mental Toughness for Success* (Houston, TX: Light Publications, 1996), p. 185.

[4] Ibid., pp. 186-87.

[5] Maxwell Maltz, *Psycho-Cybernetics* (Prentice Hall, Inc.,1960), p. vii.

[6] Ibid., p. ix.

[7] James Strong, *The New Strong's Exhaustive Concordance, Hebrew Chaldee Dictionary* (Nashville: Thomas Nelson Publishers, 1990), Entry #6754, p. 99.

[8] Ibid., Entry #1823, p. 222.

[9] *Webster's New World Dictionary, College Edition* (The World Publishing Company, USA, 1957), p. 586.

[10] Maltz, p. vii.

[11] Ibid., p. ix.

[12] Ibid., p. 2.

[13] Ibid.

[14] Ibid., p. 24.

[15] Ibid., p. 31.

[16] Ibid., p. 12.

[17] T. Harv Eker, *Secrets of the Millionaire's Mind* (New York: Harper Business, 2005), p. 107.

[18] Brian Tracy, *Change Your Thinking, Change Your Life* (Hoboken, NJ: John Wiley & Sons, Inc., 2003), p. 3.

[19] Ibid.

[20] Eker, p. 111.

[21] Gesenius, *Hebrew-Chaldee Lexicon to the Old Testament* (Grand Rapids, MI: Baker Book House Co., 1979), Entry #7181, p. 746.

[22] Lou Tice tape.

[23] Joseph H. Thayer, *Thayer's Greek-English Lexicon of the New Testament* (Grand Rapids, MI: Baker Book House, 1977), Entry # 1097, p. 117.

[24] Webster, American Dictionary of Everyday Language, p. 45; Webster, p. 1170; Strong's, *Hebrew Chaldee Dictionary*, Entry #835, p. 18; Creflo Dollar message at Mabee Center Word Explosion.

[25] Gesenius, Entry # 2556, p. 296.

[26] Strong's, *Hebrew-Chaldee Dictionary*, Entry #1897, Entry #1899, p. 32; Webster, p. 914.

[27] Byrne, p. 91.

[28] Strong's, *Hebrew Chaldee Dictionary*, Entry #7503, p. 119; Gesenius, #7503, p. 776.

[29] Brian Tracy, *Million Dollar Habits*, p. 48.

[30] Eker, pp. 166-67.

[31] Ibid., p. 167.

[32] Byrne, *The Secret*, DVD.

[33] Ibid.

CHAPTER 5

[1] Rhonda Byrne, *The Secret* (Hillsboro, OR: Atria Books, Beyond Words Publishing, 2006), p. 6.

[2] Ibid., p. 3.

[3] Ibid., p. 4.

[4] Ibid., p. 9.

[5] Ibid., p. 12.

[6] Brian Tracy, *Maximum Achievement* (New York: Simon & Schuster, 1993) p. 4.

[7] Ibid., p. 45.

[8] Ibid., p. 48.

[9] I.V. Hilliard, *Mental Toughness for Success* (Houston: Light Publications, 2003), p. 67.

[10] Tracy, p. 53.

[11] Brian Tracy, *Million Dollar Habits* (Canada: Entrepreneur Media Inc., 2004), p. 24.

[12] Joel Osteen, *Your Best Life Now* (New York: Warner Faith, Time Warner Book Group, 2004).

[13] I.V. Hilliard, *Mental Toughness for Success* (Houston, TX: Light Publications, 2003).

[14] Maxwell Maltz, *Psycho-Cybernetics* (New York: Pocket Books, 1960), p. ix.

[15] Ibid., p. 2.

[16] Ibid., p. 4.

[17] www.barna.org, Barna Update, Barna by Topic, "Stewardship," April 5, 2000.

CHAPTER 6

[1] www.inovationtools.com

[2] Joseph H. Thayer, *Thayer's Greek-English Lexicon of the New Testament,* (Baker Book House, Grand Rapids, Michigan, 1977), Entry #932, p. 96-98.

[3] James Strong, *The New Strong's Exhaustive Concordance of the Bible, Greek Dictionary of the New Testament* (Nashville: Thomas Nelson Publishers, 1984), Entry #1484, p.25. Thayer, Entry #1484, p. 169.

[4] Brian Tracy, *Create Your Own Future,* (John Wiley & Sons, Inc., Hoboken, NJ, 2002), p. 17.

[5] Ibid.

[6] Brian Tracy, *Change Your Thinking, Change Your Life* (John Wiley & Sons, Inc., Hoboken, NJ, 2003), p. 3.

[7] Harry Beckwith, *Selling the Invisible* (Warner Books, New York, 1997), p. 185.

[8] Webster, *Webster's New World Dictionary,* College Edition (The World Publishing Company, USA,1957) p.1439.

[9] Ibid, p. 799.

[10] Dr. James Richards, *Grace the Power to Change* (Whitaker House, New Kensington, PA, 1993), p. 36.

[11] Matthew 11:28-30.

[12] Strong's, *Greek Dictionary of the New Testament,* Entry #5485, p. 77. Thayer, Entry #5485, p. 666.

[13] Dr. James Richards, *Grace the Power to Change,* p. 36.

[14] Ibid, p. 70.

[15] Conversation with Dr. Jim Richards

[16] Psalm 35:27

CHAPTER 7

[1] Rhonda Byrne, *The Secret* (Hillsboro, OR: Atria Books, Beyond Words Publishing, 2006), p. 45.

[2] Ibid., p. 46.

[3] Ibid., p. 49.

[4] R. C. H. Lenski, *St. Mark's Gospel* (Minneapolis: Augsburg Publishing House, 1964), p. 493.

[5] web-site: awmi.net/bible, Mark 11:23.

[6] Ibid., Matthew 17:20.

[7] Ibid., Luke 17:7-10.

[8] Ibid., Matthew 17:3

[9] Ibid., Luke 6:52.

[10] *Webster's New World Dictionary, College Edition* (The World Publishing Company, USA, 1957), p. 659; James Strong, *The New Strong's Exhaustive Concordance* (Nashville: Thomas Nelson Publishers, 1990), Entry #4456, p. 63.

[11] Andrew Womack, *Hardness of Heart* (Colorado Springs, 1991), p. 13.

[12] Strong's, *Greek Dictionary of the New Testament,* Entry #5287, p. 75; Joseph H. Thayer, *Thayer's Greek-English Lexicon of the New Testament* (Grand Rapids, MI: Baker Book House, 1977), Entry # 5287, pp. 644-45; Webster, p. 1454; R. C. H. Lenski, *The Epistle to Hebrews and the Epistle of James* (Minneapolis: Augsburg Publishing House, 1966), p. 375.

[13] Noah Webster, *American Dictionary of the English Language*, 1st ed., (San Francisco: Foundation for American Christian Education, 2002), p. 769.

[14] Kenneth Wuest, *Word Studies in Greek N.T.,* vol. 2 (Grand Rapids: Wm. B. Eerdman Publishing Company, 1973), p. 94.

[15] Andy Andrews, *The Traveler's Gift* (Nashville: Thomas Nelson Publishers, 2002), p. 154.

[16] Ibid., p. 155.

[17] Ibid., p. 157.

[18] Derived from a conversation from someone who heard an Andrew Womack message.

[19] Womack, p. 13.

[20] Myles Munroe, *Understanding Your Potential* (Shippensburg, PA: Destiny Image, 1991), p. 145.

[21] Ibid., p. 49.

[22] Webster, *American Dictionary of the English Language*, p. 62.

[23] Jack Canfield, *The Success Principles* (New York, NY: Harper Collins Publishers, Inc., 2005), p. 35.

[24] Ibid.

[25] Ibid., p. 36.

[26] Ibid., p. 40.

[27] Ibid., p. 43.

CHAPTER 8

[1] James Canfield, *The Success Principle* (New York: Harper Collins Publishers, Inc., 2005), p. 44.

[2] James Strong, *The New Strong's Exhaustive Concordance, Greek Dictionary* (Nashville: Thomas Nelson Publishers, 1990), Entry #3126, p. 46.

[3] Gesenius, *Hebrew-Chaldee Lexicon to the Old Testament* (Grand Rapids: Baker Book House Co., 1979), Entry #6743, p. 710, Entry #7919, pp. 789-90; Webster, *Webster's New World Dictionary, College Edition* (The World Publishing Company, USA, 1957), p. 1170.

[4] Quote from message from Jerry Savelle service at Victory Christian Center, Tulsa, OK.

5 Canfield, p. 74.

6 *Webster's New World Dictionary, College Edition* (The World Publishing Company, USA, 1957), p. 215.

7 I heard the formula in a Bob Harrison Hawaii seminar in 2005.

8 Webster, p. 3.

9 Ibid., p. 1240.

10 Noah Webster, *American Dictionary of the English Language*, 1st ed. (San Francisco: Foundation for American Christian Education, 2002), p. 83.

11 Mark Victor Hansen and Robert G. Allen, *One Minute Millionaire* (New York: Harmony Books, New York, 2002), p. 58.

12 Webster, *American Dictionary,* p. 33.; Webster, *New World Dictionary,* p. 1069.

13 Brian Tracy, *Create Your Own Future* (Hoboken, NJ: John Wiley & Sons, Inc., 2002), p. 59.

14 Ibid., p. 63.

15 Myles Munroe, *The Spirit of Leadership* (New Kensington, PA: Whitaker House, 2005), p. 98.

16 Tracy, *Create Your Own Future,* p. 20.

17 Webster, p. 338.

18 Churchill.

19 Webster, p. 415.

20 Andy Stanley, *The Next Generation Leader* (Sisters, OR: Multnomah Publisher, 2003), p. 53.

21 Brian Tracy, *Change Your Thinking, Change Your Mind* (Hoboken, NJ: John Wiley & Sons, Inc., 2003), pp. 143, 144.

22 Webster, p. 1431.

23 Bob Harrison Newsletter, May, 2007.

24 Rhonda Byrne, *The Secret* (Hillsboro, OR: Atria Books, Beyond Words Publishing, 2006), p. 107.

25 Ibid.

26 Ibid., p. 103.

27 David Bach, *Start Late Finish Rich* (New York: Broadway Books, 2006), p. 7.

28 Ibid.

29 David Bach, *The Automatic Millionaire* (New York: Broadway Books, 2004), p. 97.

CHAPTER 9

1 *Webster's New World Dictionary, College Edition* (The World Publishing Company, USA, 1957), p. 1210.

2 Noah Webster, *American Dictionary of the English Language,* 1st ed., (San Francisco: Foundation for American Christian Education, 2002), p. 21.

3 Rhonda Byrne, *The Secret* (Hillsboro, OR: Atria Books, Beyond Words Publishing, 2006), p. 142.

4 Ibid., p. 143.

5 Myles Munroe, *Understanding the Purpose & Power of Prayer* (New Kensington, PA: 2002), p. 14.

6 Joseph H. Thayer, *Thayer's Greek-English Lexicon of the New Testament*, (Grand Rapids: MI, 1977), Entry #5485, p. 667.

7 James Strong, *The New Strong's Exhaustive Concordance of the Bible, Greek Dictionary of the New Testament* (Nashville: Thomas Nelson Publishers, 1984), Entry #3306, p. 47; Thayer, Entry #3306, p. 399; Webster, *New World Dictionary*, p. 3.

8 William McDonald—"governance": Dr. McDonald is a language professor at Oral Roberts University. These insights were confirmed in a conversation with him. The kingdom of heaven equates to the supernatural element of God. God's rule is primarily in the heart of man. The kingdom's rule on earth is activating God's supernatural provision by yielding to it in our hearts.

⁹ Dr. James Richards, *Grace: the Power to Change* (New Kensington, PA: Whitaker House, New Kensington, 1993), p. 36.

¹⁰ Brian Tracy, *Create Your Own Future* (Hoboken, NJ: John Wiley & Sons, Inc., 2002) p. 241.

¹¹ Noah Webster, *American Dictionary of the English Language*, 1ˢᵗ ed. (San Francisco: Foundation for American Christian Education, 2002), p. 91.

¹² Thayer, entry #1468, p. 167.

CHAPTER 10

¹ James Strong, *The New Strong's Exhaustive Concordance, Greek Dictionary of the New Testament* (Nashville: Thomas Nelson Publishers, 1990), Entry #4100, 4102, p. 58; Joseph H. Thayer, *Thayer's Greek-English Lexicon of the New Testament*, (Grand Rapids: MI, Baker Book House, 1977), Entry #4100, Entry #4102, pp. 511-14.

² Dodie Osteen, *Healed of Cancer* (Houston, TX: Lakewood Church Publication, 1986), p. 15.

³ Ibid., p. 18.

⁴ Ibid., p. 29.

⁵ Strong's, *Greek Dictionary of the New Testament*, Entry #308, Entry #309, p. 10.

ABOUT THE AUTHOR

Ron McIntosh is an international motivational speaker, author, Director of a Bible school and a consultant and coach to various organizations. His message on leadership and productivity has been heard the world over.

He is the President of Ron McIntosh Ministries and I.M.P.A.C.T., a leadership and church consulting (coaching) ministry. He is also the Executive Director of Victory Bible Institute, in Tulsa, Oklahoma.

Ron is the former Campus Pastor of Oral Roberts University and the author of the best-selling book, *The Quest for Revival*. The book has now been translated into four languages around the world. Ron serves on several boards including Impact Productions. He has been a guest of several television ministries and has a gift of exposing God's principles of leadership, productivity and revival to his generation. Ron's unique blend of insight and practical application inspires people to find the life they were born to live.

Ron has a Bachelor of Science degree in Christian Education and a Master of Divinity from Oral Roberts University. He and his wife, Judy, live in Tulsa, Oklahoma, and are the proud parents of three children; David, Daniel, and Jonathan. You can access Ron's website at www.rmmimpact.com

Additional copies of this book are available
from your local bookstore.

If this book has touched your life
we would like to hear from you.

Please write us at:

White Stone Books
P.O. Box 2835
Lakeland, Florida 33806